The Book of Lunar Oracles

Wisdom from the Goddesses of the Moon

SARAH BARTLETT

PIATKUS

PIATKUS

First published in Great Britain in 2025 by Piatkus

1 3 5 7 9 10 8 6 4 2

Copyright © Sarah Bartlett, 2025
Illustrations copyright © Sarah Bartlett and Jess Bartlett, 2025

The moral right of the author has been asserted.

A CIP catalogue record for this book
is available from the British Library.

ISBN 978-034944-190-0

Typeset in Perpetua by M Rules
Printed and bound in Great Britain by
Clays Ltd, Elcograf S.p.A.

Papers used by Piatkus are from well-managed forests
and other responsible sources.

Piatkus
An imprint of
Little, Brown Book Group
Carmelite House
50 Victoria Embankment
London EC4Y 0DZ

The authorised representative
in the EEA is
Hachette Ireland
8 Castlecourt Centre
Dublin 15, D15 XTP3, Ireland
(email: info@hbgi.ie)

An Hachette UK Company
www.hachette.co.uk

Contents

Note to Readers

Feminine and Masculine Principles

In most ancient mythology, folklore and belief systems, nature was, and still is, considered a feminine principle, as in 'Mother Nature' and 'Mother Earth'. In nature, every copse, ocean, star or cloud was also identified with, or personified as, a male or female spirit, god or goddess, and so on. I use these masculine and feminine archetypes according to tradition.

Northern and Southern Hemispheres

Please note that for the purposes of this book, I am working with the northern hemisphere; for example, the summer solstice in the northern hemisphere is around 21 June, but this would be the winter solstice for southern-hemisphere dwellers.

Similarly, in the northern hemisphere, a new crescent moon looks like an arc of light curving outwards to the right, but in the southern hemisphere a new crescent moon would be seen as an arc of light curving outwards to the left.

Name Variations and Spellings

Many of the goddesses in this book were worshipped in many different guises, sometimes with variations to their name, depending on the location and tradition. Some goddesses were merged with other deities from earlier or neighbouring traditions, and adapted according to the cultural needs of the time. This is particularly noticeable with the ancient Greek deities who were assigned new titles and assimilated into the Roman pantheon. For example, the Greek goddess, Artemis, was known to the Romans as Diana, while Selene's counterpart was Luna. Although many of these goddesses shared similar attributes, every goddess has her own unique identity, and embodies the distinct qualities of each of the forty-eight zodiac lunar energies.

Introduction

The moon has been treasured as a source of sacred power and mystical guidance since the dawn of humanity. By aligning with the moon's fluctuating rhythms and engaging with her sacred oracles, you can create a clearer picture of where you want to go and how to shape your own destiny. This book connects you not only to the mystical ebb and flow of divine lunar wisdom running deep within you, but also to the lunar goddesses' messages, to empower, inspire and bring greater insight into what really matters.

In most traditions, the moon was associated with the feminine principle, so for the purposes of this book, the many voices of the moon – her lunar oracles – are represented by goddesses, enchant-resses, sibyls and other mythical feminine characters who embody the qualities and energies associated with the transiting moon across the year, giving a total of forty-eight oracles. These characters include goddesses from many worldwide traditions, such as Selene, Persephone, Mama Killa, Lilith and Rhiannon; enchantresses and nymphs such as Ceridwen, Circe, the Vila; and those characters known for their prophetic power, like the Sybil and Hecate. It is their voices that will guide, invite, remind or gently direct you, revealing what you need to know, express or reflect upon.

This book is a complete oracle guide for spiritual and personal growth. It is not intended to help you predict the future as such, but to offer direction and guidance on how to make appropriate choices so that your future can be what you want it to be.

The book can be approached in a variety of ways:

- for support, direction or guidance on a particular question or situation
- for self-reflection and meditation
- for cultivating self-knowledge, self-belief and authenticity
- to help you make choices for a meaningful life
- to encourage you to live in harmony with the changing cycles of the moon.

By connecting with these lunar feminine archetypes, you can live more authentically and actively make choices for **what you need to know at this moment in time** and to understand the deeper truth of who you are and where you are going.

Whether you call on the goddesses to answer a question, cultivate self-knowledge or align yourself with the lunar energy of the day in question, this book is a sacred mirror of all that you are.

Look in this book as you would look in a mirror, for it is a book of you.

Consulting the Oracles

The book has been designed to be used like a set of oracle cards. The oracles are set out in no particular order, so you can randomly flick through the pages, or open the book by chance, just as you would randomly draw a card after shuffling the deck.

Before consulting the oracles, try to find a quiet place where you won't be disturbed. Take a few moments to settle into stillness and calm, and perhaps light a tea-light candle for atmosphere. You might want to close your eyes, and open your mind to your intuition, or if you have a burning question, focus on that for a moment or two.

I'm going to share my favourite ways to use this book, but they are by no means the only ways. As always, follow your intuition and go with whatever feels right for you.

A treasure trove of lunar wisdom

You may want to read this book to better understand feminine lunar wisdom and to discover the myths surrounding the lunar goddesses it references, what they mean to you, and how they relate to your own life. Simply read through the ones that take your fancy, dip in and out, or read from beginning to end, and let the moon's oracles take you on a journey of self-knowledge.

Inspiration, Divination and Self-reflection

Close your eyes, hold a question in your mind, then pick up this book and pause for a few moments as you connect with the oracles. Open the book, or flick through the pages with your eyes closed, stopping when you feel intuitively the moment is right. Read the lunar oracle on the page you land on, and relate it to your question, or how it might feel relevant to what is going on in your life right now. If you land on an illustrated page, read the associated goddess entry. Use this same method if you don't have a question and just want to see what comes up.

Intentional Choice

Choose a goddess whose attributes you would like to invoke, work with or embody right now. Maybe also consider if the goddess is choosing you, telling you this is a time to align with her qualities? Is she reaching out to you to empower you with beneficial wisdom?

If you are seeking daily guidance that corresponds to the current lunar phase, first check in an almanac, ephemeris or online what zodiac sign and phase the moon is in. For example, if you discover the full moon is in Capricorn, turn to the index at the back of the book and find the relevant goddess and page number, and then read her message. Consider what this means to you today and how it may manifest in your life right now.

If you're seeking an answer to a specific question, and it's covered by one of the three themed oracles (Romantic Relationships, Future Purpose, and Family, Friends and Home Life), choose a goddess that you feel an intuitive connection with (this will likely change each time you consult this book). You can also turn to the goddess who corresponds to the current lunar phase for the same reason.

What to Ask?

You may want to consider one of the follow questions as you hold this book:

- What do I need to know right now?
- What would I like to manifest in my life?
- What needs to be brought to light?
- What am I seeking?
- Where am I going?

Experiment, trust your intuition, and most of all enjoy interacting with these lunar voices who have your best interests at heart – because, after all, they are at the heart and soul of you.

Part 1

Understanding the Power of the Moon

Before you delve into the oracles, it's useful to know some facts about the moon and her oracles and to understand how mythology is intertwined in this empowering lunar flow.

The Lunar Cycle and Astrology

The Zodiac

There are two different zodiac systems in use by astrologers. **The Tropical Zodiac**, which is measured by the apparent pathway of the sun as it appears to travel round the Earth (an imaginary belt known as the ecliptic), is made up of twelve zodiac signs of 30 degrees each, forming a 360-degree circle. The Tropical Zodiac always begins with Aries at zero degrees and the vernal equinox. **The Sidereal Zodiac** (used in Vedic astrology) is also made up of twelve signs but is calculated against the backdrop of the current position of the stars and constellations, which changes over the years. For the purposes of this book, I am using the Tropical Zodiac.

Lunar Cycle

The lunar cycle refers to the time it takes for the moon to make one orbit around the zodiac along the ecliptic, taking approximately twenty-nine days.

Lunar Phase

Each lunar phase is determined by the angle of the moon in relation to the sun, and the amount of sunlight falling on the moon.

For example, when we talk about a **full moon** in Aries, this is when the sun is in the sign of Libra (September/October) and the moon is directly opposite the sun or 180 degrees away from it (Aries is the opposite sign to Libra). The moon is then lit up completely (from our viewpoint on Earth) by the sun's light.

A **dark of the new moon** in Aries is when the sun and the moon are conjunct – i.e. at the same degree of Aries. The moon is now between the Earth and the sun, making the moon's surface impossible to see from our geocentric view. A dark of the new moon in Aries will therefore occur in March/April, when the sun is in Aries.

The most commonly known lunar phases are:

WAXING MOON

From the first fine sliver of a crescent of light, visibly curving outwards, it gradually increases to half a circle, then a complete circle of light – the full moon.

Keywords: progress, inspiration, motivation, boldness, vitality, talent, creativity.

FULL MOON

This is when the moon's face is completely lit up. Once the moon reaches her maximum culmination or fullest light, she then begins to lose it.

Keywords: receptivity, mothering, productivity, wellbeing, completion, success, fulfilment.

WANING MOON

After the full moon phase, the moon gradually diminishes to a half-full circle, until she eventually appears as a tiny sliver of a crescent before she disappears completely – the dark of the new moon.

Keywords: acceptance, untying, reappraisal, relinquishment, review, release.

DARK OF THE NEW MOON

This is when the moon is invisible from Earth, due to her close proximity to the sun. She will then become a fine crescent waxing moon again and we are back to the start of the cycle.

Keywords: mystique, intuition, wildness, spirituality, magic, transformation, enchantment.

Mythology and the Moon

In most worldwide mythology, the moon was, and still is, associated with the feminine principle (i.e. mother/maiden/crone, creativity, receptivity, darkness, mystery) and is embodied by the goddesses and mythical figures who represent her. Similarly, the sun is associated with the masculine principle: light, adventure, willpower and ego. Although moon gods do appear in some traditions such as Inuit, Semitic and Japanese, lunar goddesses outnumber them overall.

What Is an Oracle?

An oracle is not only a message sent from a deity in answer to a specific question, or to prophesy the future, but it can also refer to the person who actually voices or channels the message. For thousands of years, we have received oracular messages from gods and goddesses of all traditions. The best-documented oracles or channellers were the Ancient Greek prophetesses known as sibyls, with the Pythia – the high priestess of Apollo's temple in Delphi – the most well known.

The person consulting the oracle would be expected to interpret the message, usually spoken as an ambiguous phrase, riddle or verse. Some oracles, such as the Erythraean and Cumaean sibyls (see page 238), wrote their messages on oak leaves in the form of an acrostic, in which the first letter of each line spells out a hidden word. A body of utterances written in hexameter verse, known as the Sibylline Oracles, was passed down through a line of Greek sibyls, eventually becoming highly prized prophecies consulted by the Roman senate (see page 238).

I have drawn on myths and lore from around the world to bring together this collection of archetypal mythical feminine characters who reflect the diverse aspects of lunar energy. However, there are many who have not been included due to space constraints or a lack of documented information to give them credit. So, if your favourite lunar representative is not included, please don't take this personally!

Now is the time to trust in and dance to the rhythm of the moon and her many voices, as she leads you along the pathway to a fulfilling life. So why not dive into the book at random, and begin?

Part 2

The Oracles

The mythological goddesses, enchantresses and sibyls in this book represent the qualities of the moon's changing energy. It is from their divine wisdom that the lunar oracles are derived. They are presented in no particular order so that the book can be used like a deck of oracle cards. Each goddess or character aligns with one of the four main phases of the moon (waxing, full, waning and dark of the new moon – see pages 3–4) as it transits each of the twelve signs of the zodiac. In astrological terms, the qualities associated with each zodiac sign have an added influence on the energy of these lunar phases. For example, a waxing moon in Aries is a time to win, achieve and promote oneself, while a waning phase in Aries is associated with overcoming setbacks and gaining new insight. A full moon in Scorpio evokes feelings of intense passion, while a full moon in Libra promotes grace and serenity. Each combination of moon phase and zodiac sign has its own unique flavour.

Each entry includes:

- A list of the goddess attributes, tradition, lunar phase and keywords, followed by a key oracle for reflection or to relate to your current situation
- The myth of the goddess, the background and her character
- Her meaning and wisdom to help you understand your current situation
- Her message
- A brief ritual to invoke her blessing
- Three themed oracles to inform: Romantic Relationships, Life Purpose, and Family, Friends and Home Life

The Four Lunar Phases

Waxing Moon Oracles

The waxing moon is a time of creativity, new experiences and fresh discoveries, and this collection of oracles is brought to you by motivated, self-assured goddesses and mythological characters who embody the moon's energising qualities during this phase. The Thracian goddess Bendis may invite you to be ready to act upon your desires, or you may discover your own inner authority with the help of the Celtic warrior goddess, the Morrígan. Allow them to help express these qualities in your life.

The twelve waxing moon goddesses:

Artemis

Awilix
Bendis
Chang'e
Diana
Hina
Isis
Medb
Rhiannon
The Morrígan
The Sibyl
The Vila

Full Moon Oracles

The full moon phase is often considered to be the most influential phase of the lunar cycle, enchanting artists, poets and writers with its magical glow. There is something empowering and ethereal about this great silver orb in the sky, so it's hardly surprising that it has also been thought to be the most auspicious time to cast spells or draw down lunar energy in esoteric and pagan belief systems. This lunar phase is connected to fulfilment, finalising plans or committing yourself to a project or relationship, so these oracles are concerned with self-empowerment and a sense of completion and wholeness. The moon's messages come to you through the voices of the goddesses and mythological characters who represent or embody these full-moon qualities. You may reclaim your passion with Selene or discover prosperity with Mama Killa. If you open the book to any of the oracles in this lunar phase, then the qualities associated with the full moon may need to be expressed or made manifest in your life.

The twelve full moon goddesses:

Arianrhod
Brigid
Britomartis
Dewi Ratih
Gaia
Hanwi
Luna
Mama Killa
Nut
Selene
Triple Goddess
Yèmọja

Waning Moon Oracles

The enchantresses, goddesses and mythological characters who represent the waning moon's diminishing energy are here to help you release or banish bad feelings, let go of the past, reflect, redefine and readjust your vision so that you are ready to move forward. These oracles also reinforce qualities that are often hidden within us, or that gradually diminish from our conscious awareness, rather like the waning moon's light. So, whether you choose an oracle by intention or chance, here you can follow the beguiling dance of the Hindu goddess Mohini, keep your secrets safe with the power of Frigg or be ready to plant your seeds of renewal when the moment is right by listening to Ixchel's words. If you are drawn to any of the oracles associated with the waning moon, it is likely that the qualities unique to this lunar cycle may need to be expressed or made manifest in your life.

The twelve waning moon goddesses:

Calypso
Devana
Dido
Frigg
Ishtar
Ix Chel
Mélusine
Morgan le Fay
Nimue
Pasiphaë
Tārā
Thetis

Dark of the New Moon Oracles

The dark of the new moon phase is a time of mystery, illusion, hidden truths and latent potential. This collection of oracles is delivered by goddesses, enchantresses or mythological characters who embody or symbolise the dark moon's qualities. These oracles also relate to our own shadowy side and how we can unfold deeper truths that aren't often brought to light. So, if you land on one of these oracles, it might be an indication that something within you needs to be expressed right now. For example, you may need to do a little soul-searching with Mesopotamian goddess Inanna, learn defiance with liberated Lilith, or understand your mystery with Greek goddess of the night, Nyx.

The twelve dark of the new moon goddesses:

Blodeuwedd
Ceridwen
Circe
Coyolxāuhqui
Hecate
Inanna
Kali
Lilith
Mohini
Nyx
Persephone
The Cailleach

Bendis

Tradition: Thracian
Symbols: spear, torch, wild animals, horses
Lunar cycle: waxing moon in Cancer
Sacred crystals: moonstone, angelite, rainbow
  obsidian
Keywords: subtle motivation, ingenuity, astute
  awareness

Key

Artfulness.

Oracle

Nothing can hold you back. This is a time to be ready for action and for knowing that success lies in the art of being elegantly understated.

Myth

Bendis, the Thracian goddess of the moon and hunting, was often depicted accompanied by nymphs, satyrs, wild beasts and maenads (the female followers of Dionysus). Bendis is an intriguing and enigmatic ancient deity whose name comes from a Proto-Indo-European root meaning 'to bind'. There is much debate as to whether this means to bind as in to tame or capture or refers to binding together in sexual union.

In early Greek art, Bendis can be seen wearing a short tunic, cloak, boots and a pointed Phrygian cap and holding a spear. According to one ancient source, she was given an epithet of *Dilonchos*, meaning 'the Goddess with the Double Spear'. This was thought either to refer to her being of both Heaven and Earth, or referring to the sun and moon, both of which emanated from her inner light.

When her worship was first introduced to Athens, she was associated with Artemis, Hecate and Selene, but her own temple was retained separately at Piraeus (the port of Athens). She became so popular during the 4th century BCE that a festival known as the Bendideia (thought to have originally included orgiastic rites and erotic dancing associated with Dionysus) was dedicated to her and celebrated in Greece with night-time torch-races on horseback.

Meaning and Wisdom

Bendis is believed to have been celebrated for fertility, protection and good fortune, but it is her silent motivational wisdom that reveals her true power. Like Artemis, Diana, Hecate and Selene, she is a goddess of the night – of moonlight, shadowy forests and woods where beasts roam. Magic abounds under the light of the moon. She comes to remind you that, like the subtle power of the waxing moon in Cancer, motivation doesn't have to be overt, you don't have to sing your praises or push others out of your way to achieve success. In fact, in Bendis we see that to be a little restrained, a little artful, and not give too much away, is more empowering than pretension and self-importance.

Her Message

Bendis asks you to consider why you have been motivated to set a current intention or goal. Perhaps you were guided by a deep inner belief or a gut feeling or felt that someone else had an influence over your decision. Have you affirmed to yourself that this is the right direction to go in, and does this intuitively feel like the right path for you? Ask yourself these questions, honestly and without self-reproach. Take Bendis's subtle approach; be gentle but firm with yourself and others, put forward your plan, let go of worry and doubt, and you will move on to the next stage of your journey. Bendis was accepted into Greek culture, but she was still true to her Thracian identity, so likewise be yourself, because no one does that better.

To Invoke Bendis's Lunar Blessing

Call on Bendis to bless future goals by repeating the following sacred words as you gaze upwards towards the moon:

> *Oh, silent moon in darkest skies,*
> *Affirm my quest is always nigh.*

I tread most carefully, step by step,
And soon will dance the pathway best.
Thank you, Bendis, for your blessing and for clarifying my
  goals.

Themed Oracles

ROMANTIC RELATIONSHIPS

There is much that still needs to be said, but you are beginning to find the courage to speak up and clear the air. Now's the time to say your piece, with pride but without hubris, with self-confidence but without arrogance, and with love but without giving all of yourself away.

LIFE PURPOSE

A desire to change things in your life may be due to external influence. Before you act on impulse, stir a little realism into the mix and see how to make the goal work for you alone, rather than work for others with no reward.

FAMILY, FRIENDS AND HOME LIFE

Something is niggling at you when it comes to your family, social circle or home. Something is telling you that all may not be what it seems and you may have to take steps to leave a situation behind. But wherever you go, your true friends will go with you. The change may also be within you rather than a literal move, but either way, take it one step at a time.

Nut

Tradition: Egyptian
Symbols: cow, sky, cosmos, water-pot, day and
    night, stars
Lunar cycle: full moon in Cancer
Sacred crystals: lapis lazuli, turquoise, red carnelian
Keywords: self-value, altruism, comfort,
    self-assurance

Key

Protection.

Oracle

From this star-filled sky, I, Nut, come to protect you.
Reach out now and you will feel my gentleness. Taste
the salted sea on the wind, see the moon rise through
my star-spangled body. You are protected, whatever the
outcome of your quest; be safe and use your personal
defences to work for you, rather than against you.

Myth

In ancient Egyptian mythology, Nut was the goddess of the night sky and some sources say the personification of the Milky Way. Usually depicted as a naked woman arched above the Earth, her hands and feet resting at either end of the horizon, her body was decorated with the stars shining through her. In later Egyptian tradition, she was goddess of the night sky, day sky, cosmos, stars, mothering and the universe.

Nut was the daughter of the primordial Egyptian gods: Shu, god of wind and air, and Tefnut, goddess of rain and moisture. Her brother and consort was Geb, the Earth. Nut held the sky in place and when Nut and Geb were born, they held each other so tightly that Nut couldn't give birth to any children. Their father eventually forced them apart to allow the next generation of gods to be born.

A different myth, detailed by the Greek historian Plutarch, suggested that the sun god, Ra, had expected Nut to be his wife. When he learned that she and Geb were lovers, he put a curse on her so she couldn't give birth to a child on any day in the year. Nut consulted Thoth, the god of wisdom, who challenged the moon god, Khonsu, to a gambling game. Every time Khonsu lost the game, he had to give Nut a piece of his moonlight. Khonsu lost so many times that Nut had enough moonlight to make five extra days. Since these days were not part of the calendar year, Nut was able to have her children. These were Osiris, god of the afterlife; Horus, god of war; Set, god of disorder and violence; Isis, goddess of magic; and Nephthys, goddess of water. When Ra found out he was enraged and separated Nut from Geb for eternity. Yet she still shines down her protective power on all.

Meaning and Wisdom

Nut was also the goddess who protected the dead when they entered the afterlife and the inside lids of sarcophagi were often painted the dark blue of the night sky in her honour. She was known as 'coverer of the sky' and 'she who protects'. In her dual role as protectress of the sun and moon, who were reborn through her every day, she covered the Earth, protecting it from the darkness beyond. Nut aligns with the full moon in Cancer phase, when the moon is at her most powerful mother aspect, enveloping us with a sense of belonging. Nut reminds us of our own protective powers of self-value and self-assurance, but also shows us that we are protected by the universe and our place in it, and that we belong.

Her Message

Nut comes to cloak you in the stars of self-belief, altruism and, mostly, self-love. Have you recently felt vulnerable, unloved or stressed by people around you? If so, now is the time to heal yourself, devoting time to hugging yourself, just as Nut wraps her arms around the Earth and embraces the moon and stars in her dark cloak. Wrap your arms around yourself and imagine the great protectress of the night cloaking you with a million stars.

To Invoke Nut's Lunar Blessing

To ask Nut to help protect you always, gaze up to the heavens at night and say:

> Nut, *who covers all by day and night,*
> *In the darkness we see you best,*
> *Your stars, your moon, your Milky Way,*
> *Please protect my life with the stars that heal and the*
>   *cosmos that cares*

End your invocation by blowing her a kiss and she will return her blessing.

Themed Oracles

ROMANTIC RELATIONSHIPS

You need to protect your interests. Perhaps your feelings or even the property or possessions you own? Whatever is relevant right now, don't give anything away. Give all of your love to yourself and protect what is dear to you.

LIFE PURPOSE

Gamble with an idea, take a risk, but make sure you know the stakes before you do so. There is much to lose, but much more to gain if you play the game honourably. Don't let anyone or anything know of your future plans until you are about to manifest them.

FAMILY, FRIENDS AND HOME LIFE

Some friends or family are in need of security, protection or advice, but it's not up to you alone to provide that. All you can offer right now is your care and reassurance, but very soon all will change for the better.

Mama Killa

Tradition: Incan
Symbols: silver, rain, serpent, mountain lion, fox
Lunar cycle: full moon in Aries
Sacred crystals: tiger's eye, obsidian, citrine
Keywords: fecundity, fruitfulness, abundance, fertility

Key

Abundance.

Oracle

Nurture the abundance of all that you are: the still waters of the soul that belie hidden undercurrents or the fertile mind that hides resolute self-belief. Plentiful ideas and pathways are about to open up for you.

Myth

Beautiful moon goddess Mama Killa (also known as Mama Quilya, Mother Moon, and Mama Kilya) was the daughter of the creator god Wiraqucha and the sea goddess Mama Qucha. Her brother and consort was the sun god, Inti, and her sister was the Earth goddess Pachamama. Her offspring included the weaving goddess Mama Uqllu and the fire god Manqu Quhapaq. Associated with fertility and abundance, Mama Killa was said to cry tears of silver, which fell as rain to nourish the Earth. As the goddess of menstruation, marriage, fertility and protection, her sacred temple at Cusco was dedicated to women. The Incas believed that lunar eclipses occurred when the goddess was being attacked by a serpent or, according to some accounts, a mountain lion. Fearful that she would be devoured and time would come to an end (the Incan agricultural calendar was dependent on the moon's cycle), the Incans attempted to scare away any predators by banging drums, making loud noises or throwing weapons. The dark spots on the moon were thought in one myth to be caused by a fox who fell in love with Mama Killa. When the fox finally reached her, she squeezed him so tightly that the marks of his body were left upon her.

Meaning and Wisdom

When Mama Killa appears in your life, she reminds you of the fertility of mind, body and spirit. She is a giver of life, the bringer of rain and protectress of precious metals (offerings of silver and gold were made at her temples) and was worshipped to ensure good harvests. Without the moon's changing face, the Incas' reliance on agriculture would be threatened. Mama Killa reminds us of our own ability to bounce back from an eclipse of the heart or a bad phase in our own lives and tells us that deep within we have the power to survive the threat of others, such as those who blame, reproach or manipulate us. The full moon in Aries phase consolidates our motivation and gives us a hefty dollop of courage to do our own thing. Mama Killa shows how she was strong enough to remain invulnerable during attacks from the serpent or the lion, and that resilience is found in her constancy and her abundant goodness.

Her Message

Mama Killa comes to ask, what does abundance mean to you? How much can you have and how much are you able to share? Abundance can mean having more than you actually need, or it can mean having an ample quantity. Do you never have enough time, or do you have too much time on your hands? Mama Killa asks you to reflect on the difference between having too much and not having enough. Mostly, she tells you to open up to the abundance of the universe and see that it is not only all around you but flows through you too. This sense of being at one with the moon, the sun and the stars, means that you can ask for more of what you need, draw it to you, and not resent others because they may appear to have more than you.

To Invoke Mama Killa's Lunar Blessing

Sit beside a white tea-light candle that will represent the moon and reflect on how, if you were to blow or snuff out the flame, it would be similar to an eclipse. Darkness would blot out the light, but because you know that this is a passing phase and that the moonlight will return very soon, you have nothing to fear. Similarly, you will always find abundance if you know that it is out there waiting for you. Thank Mama Killa for her gifts and she will reward you with what you truly need to feel abundant.

Themed Oracles

ROMANTIC RELATIONSHIPS

Don't regret or feel bitter about what you don't have, instead nurture what you do have, even if you aren't in a relationship. You are in relationship with yourself, so love yourself as you would another.

LIFE PURPOSE

The manifestation of your goal or current quest is in sight and with plentiful ideas you can now start to make the right kind of contacts to give you the support and advice you need.

FAMILY, FRIENDS AND HOME LIFE

It would be nice to have more than you already have, a bigger home perhaps, a larger family, or just a feeling that the glass is half full, rather than half empty. Soon you will have just the right amount that you need to feel in balance again.

Kali

Tradition: Hindu
Symbols: honey, hibiscus or jasmine perfume or
   flowers, dance
Lunar cycle: dark of the moon in Scorpio
Sacred crystals: black tourmaline, sodalite, azurite
Keywords: time, change, endings and
   beginnings, hope

Key

Change.

Oracle

There is only one constant in life and that is change. If you dare to change your mind or change your perception of how your life could be, everything will change for the better.

Myth

In Hindu belief, Kali (meaning time) is the embodiment of the divine feminine power known as Shakti. She is depicted with blue or black skin, a tongue covered with blood, a skirt made of dismembered limbs and a human skull necklace. Yet Kali is as much a protectress as she is a destroyer. In one myth, a terrible undefeated demon, Raktabīja, was wreaking havoc on the world. The goddess of war, Durga, tried to destroy him on the battlefield but she soon realised that every time the demon was wounded and a droplet of his blood touched the ground, a duplicate of him would spring forth. Faced with the threat of the demon and his countless doubles, Durga summoned Kali, who was born out of her forehead. Kali was able to unroll her tongue across the battlefield and use it to consume the demon and all of his duplicates. She then performed a victory dance so frenzied that it threatened to crack open the Earth. The god Shiva, seeing the planet was in danger, lay prostrate to protect it. When Kali realised she was about to trample him into the ground, she stopped her dance and became the protectress of the Earth.

Kali is a paradox: she is the goddess of darkness, destruction and death, but is also creative and nurturing. Her many manifestations and myths appear throughout the varying belief systems of Hindu-based religion in India and South Asia. Yet wherever Kali is, she takes us out of our darkness to help us address our resistance to change and bring to light our own values.

Meaning and Wisdom

Kali dances wildly into your life, to tell you it's time to address your dark thoughts, doubts or wounds that have never healed. In fact, Kali is there to consume your pain, like she did the demon, so that you are free from the things that hurt you. Kali reminds us that we are always going to be challenged in life, but if we face our fear of challenge, we can dance through that too and reach the place beyond. Like the dark of the moon in Scorpio, Kali tells us that transformation is about accepting that the only thing in life that is constant is change itself. Sometimes this transformative power, however seemingly threatening or unwelcome, can bring the best of us to life.

Her Message

To align with Kali's transformative power, ask yourself: am I fearful of living life to the full? If so, why? What's stopping you? Are you manipulated by the demons of social media, or the expectations and the wishes of others? Are you fearful of shedding the things that haven't materialised as you'd hoped, or a dream that never came true? It's time to liberate yourself from the clanking skulls around your neck and dance courage, fresh hope and transformative power into your life. See how goodness can come forth from the darkest of places.

To Invoke Kali's Lunar Blessing

You can repeat this verse to Kali or any other you prefer, then sweep your arms up to the moon to draw down her lunar energy and invoke her blessing.

> *I chance, I choose, I challenge now,*
> *I dance, I view, I change no vow.*
> *To Kali, bring me fearless change*
> *This moonlit night for love and gain.*

Then thank Kali for her dance of change and acknowledge that change is progress.

Themed Oracles

ROMANTIC RELATIONSHIPS

A change is imminent. Kali tells you that it's time to rekindle an old relationship or take a chance on a new relationship. Honour change for what it is: a turning point and a new departure.

LIFE PURPOSE

You're managing to let go of unrealistic projects and impractical dreams, and you're hungry for something to take their place. This is your chance to tap into your creativity and to allow something beautiful to blossom from it.

FAMILY, FRIENDS AND HOME LIFE

There may be changes afoot – some that are welcome and some that are not. But the more you resist that change, the more someone will try to put pressure on you for answers. Make it clear you are going to follow your intuition on this, not their holier-than-thou attitude.

Dewi Ratih

Tradition: Hindu (worshipped in Java and Bali)
Symbols: fruit, rice grains, flower petals,
   sandalwood incense
Sacred crystals: pearl, opal
Lunar cycle: full moon in Libra
Keywords: beauty, empathy, generosity,
   self-possession

Key

Grace.

Oracle

**Even if you've felt overwhelmed or consumed with other
people's worries, you are about to see that your grace,
beauty and self-possession will shine through the darkness and return you to light.**

Myth

The Hindu goddess of the moon in Balinese and Javan mythology,
Dewi Ratih, was renowned for her beauty. She was much desired

by Kala Rau, the king of a race of demonic giants who lived on Earth. But Dewi Ratih rejected the giant's advances and in his revenge, he planned to devour her. Kala Rau pretended to be a god himself so he could get close to her in the sky. To make sure he was immortal, he found the gods' elixir of immortality, *amrita*, and began to drink a little. But Dewi Ratih had already warned the lord of the gods, Vishnu, of the giant's intentions towards her, and as the liquid touched the back of his throat, Vishnu beheaded Kalu Rau. His decapitated head survived in the sky because he had tasted the *amrita* and his head continued to chase Dewi Ratih across the heavens. Every so often he caught up with her, and would swallow her whole, but because he had no body, Dewi Ratih could free herself. Each time she was swallowed, the moon disappeared, and this story was thought to be the cause of a lunar eclipse. In Bali, a ceremony is held every *pūrṇimā* (full moon) to celebrate and appease the gods and to connect with Dewi Ratih's beauty.

Meaning and Wisdom

Dewi Ratih represents the grace and beauty within all of us that shines through even when we are consumed by our own demons. In fact, like the harmonious influence of the full moon in Libra, she tells you to be calm amid the choppy waters of your sea of troubles, and in doing so you will find your way to shore again. Just like when we understand what a lunar eclipse actually is, we know there's nothing to fear because after darkness comes the return of the light. For every dark experience of our own, there is a bright one to follow.

Her Message

This is a time to affirm your self-worth and to celebrate your inner grace. Dewi Ratih reminds you that if you don't yet see or value the beauty within yourself, then it's time to start doing so. Maybe stop comparing yourself to others or trends, and trust in yourself more. Beauty and grace come from within – you don't need to try to look like or emulate anyone else. True elegance and composure come from simply being yourself. Don't eclipse your beauty, express it.

To Invoke Dewi Ratih's Lunar Blessing

Burn sandalwood incense or lay out seasonal fruits and flowers on a table to connect with Dewi Ratih's graceful presence. To invoke her blessing simply say, 'Dewi Ratih, with your goodness and grace, listen to my prayers and wishes, and help me to radiate my true charisma and beauty.'

Themed Oracles

ROMANTIC RELATIONSHIPS

A dark period or an eclipse of the heart is coming to an end. It's time to find romance again and enjoy gracing your relationship with warmth and heartfelt gratitude for who you are and what you have.

LIFE PURPOSE

What seemed like an impossible goal is now beginning to look possible. Choose the people who choose you and you will start to make the impact you intended.

FAMILY, FRIENDS AND HOME LIFE

Graciously accept that others have to follow their own path. But if this creates conflict, now is the time to speak up and make it clear that your own choices are just as important as theirs. Agree to accept your differences.

Awilix

Tradition: Mayan
Symbols: rain, springs, sea, rivers, rabbit
Lunar Cycle: waxing moon in Capricorn
Sacred crystals: ruby, garnet, moonstone
Keywords: fertility, kindness, giving, benevolence

Key

Generosity.

Oracle

Be kind to yourself, to nature, to all around you and connect with the seasons. The generosity you give out will come back to brighten your life.

Myth

Awilix (also spelt Ahuilix, Auilix and Avilix) was a Mayan goddess of the moon and was associated with sexuality, procreation, fertility and growth. She also governed all forms of water, whether rain, springs, wells, seas or rivers. Although in some myths the sun is her consort, in others she is the grandmother, or sometimes mother, of the sun. The lunar rabbit associated with depictions of Awilix is thought to be either one of her children transformed into a rabbit, or a rabbit responsible for destroying the vegetation in the sun god's maize field. In the second version of the myth, the rabbit was eventually captured by the sun god and given to Awilix, who took it to live with her in the sky. In north-western Guatemala, the rabbit in the moon is sometimes replaced by a deer, while in ancient Mayan art, Awilix is shown as a young woman holding a rabbit, framed by a crescent waxing moon.

Meaning and Wisdom

Although little is known about Awilix, her association with the rabbit invites us to consider her most common role as a goddess of nature, the moon and the seasons. Similarly, across many different cultures worldwide, the rabbit is a symbol of fertility, abundance and regeneration. Rabbits also represent spring and new beginnings and were thought by many traditions to be associated with the cyclical nature of the moon. In many Asian and Native American cultures, the dark markings seen on the moon were identified as the shape of a rabbit, who disappeared (marking the dark of the new moon) then returned with the gradual waxing to full moon phase. The moon's phases also align to one of Awilix's earliest identities as goddess of the female menstrual cycle. Her motherly, kind and gentle character is revealed in the story where she looks after the rabbit. Her embracing, giving nature aligns to the energy of the waxing moon in Capricorn, when there is a sense of generosity, a feeling of comfort, safety, traditional togetherness and collective harmony. So, alongside Awilix, the rabbit is safe and her benevolence shines down on us every time we glimpse the moon.

Her Message

The mysterious Awilix comes to tell you that now is the time to be more generous towards others, yourself and the natural world. It's time to give without asking for anything back, to show your appreciation for your own and other people's talents or strengths. Like Awilix, who didn't judge the rabbit for his natural propensity to dig up a maize field, you will discover the joy in loving others without conditions, expectations or judgement, and for accepting others for who they are. Hers is a pathway to being generous with your praise and, as you do so, finding peace with others and the gift of loving kindness returned to you.

To Invoke Awilix's Lunar Blessing

Step out into the countryside and, whether it's raining, sunny or a misty day, reach up to the sky with both arms as if to embrace the rabbit and the moon, for Awilix is always there, tenderly holding her rabbit and caring for the natural world. If you show you care for nature – wildlife, seasons, rain or moon – then she will send you her blessing too.

Themed Oracles

ROMANTIC RELATIONSHIPS

Being generous in a relationship is the way to move forward, but it is both generosity to yourself, and the care and attention you pay to someone else, that will determine your future.

LIFE PURPOSE

The more you give attention to what is being said, the more you will find that things evolve as you would like them to. It's not so much that you are ignoring others' opinions, but perhaps you need to listen and learn before you make any value judgements.

FAMILY, FRIENDS AND HOME LIFE

You have friends or family who could help you go far in your ambitions, but you just need a little more courage and self-confidence to ask for their advice. Do yourself a favour for once, and they may well do you a favour too.

Gaia

Tradition: Ancient Greek
Symbols: the Earth, plants, wildlife, cosmos, mother
Lunar cycle: full moon in Taurus
Sacred crystals: emerald, green tourmaline, malachite
Keywords: hope, abundance, gratitude, resolution, commitment

Key

Promise.

Oracle

All that is born from the Earth is born from deep within you; all that is promised, cherished and nurtured within is about to bring abundance to you.

Myth

One of the most well-known Earth goddesses of ancient mythology, Gaia (or Gaea) is the archetypal Earth Mother in Western mythology. As the personification of the Earth itself, she arose from Chaos (the void), along with Eros (the god of love), Nyx (night) and Erebus (darkness). With her son, the god of the heavens, Uranus, she gave birth to the Titans, as well as the Cyclopes and the Hundred-Handed giants. For fear of being overpowered, Uranus forced their offspring to remain hidden in the depths of the Earth – Gaia herself. Gaia was furious and secretly asked her children to help her overthrow their father, but only the Titan, Cronus, was willing to do so. Gaia fashioned a diamond sickle and told Cronus to hide beside their bed and when Uranus came to lie with her, castrate his father. Cronus did exactly that, casting the severed testicles into the sea. The castrated Uranus lost all his power and with Cronus as leader, the Titans went on to rule Heaven and Earth, until their own children, the Olympians, took over.

Gaia had many lovers, mostly her sons and brothers, and birthed a range of monsters, such as the serpentine giant, Typhon. With her Titan son, Oceanus, she produced the Fates; with her grandson, Poseidon, she produced Charybdis, the dreaded sea monster that Odysseus faced, and there were many who were born without known fathers, such as the Sirens. Gaia was not only an Earth and mother goddess, but she was also the first oracle goddess at Delphi, where her cult centre was guarded by her son, the serpent Python.

Meaning and Wisdom

As the personification of Earth's abundance, Gaia is associated with the Earth-Mother energy of the full moon in Taurus. She is the embodiment of planet Earth and brought all of life into being. Aligning to Gaia's lunar phase encourages us to hope and believe in abundance; we realise we can make and keep promises and we can give freely and demand little back. Gaia is like the committed voice in the oracle cave, the unstoppable wind as it whistles through your hair and the unmoving ground on which you tread. She is in you and around you, and as you gaze at the moon from Gaia's Earth, you know the lunar light shines down on you with her blessing.

Her Message

Gaia reminds you that you are made of this Earth and all of the universe. You are physical, sensual, sexual and fertile of mind, body and heart, and now is the time to discover a way to give life to your creative thoughts. Gaia reminds you that deep within you have the belief, the integrity and the will to succeed and to create abundance and good fortune in your life. Promise yourself you will achieve one long-term goal and then start to put your goal into action.

To Invoke Gaia's Lunar Blessing

When you have the opportunity to get out into nature, sit on the ground cross-legged or whatever feels most comfortable for you. Close your eyes and focus on the solid ground beneath your sit bones. Imagine that roots run deep down from where you sit into the core of the Earth. Place both your hands on the ground and say, 'I am at one with the Earth, the moon, the sun and all of the universe. Thank you, Gaia, for your abundance.'

Themed Oracles

ROMANTIC RELATIONSHIPS

Gaia gives you the chance to make a promise, a commitment to your future, or to honour the bond with a romantic partner. This is an important turning point, so don't doubt yourself: act now.

LIFE PURPOSE

Life is for doing things, not dreaming about them. Don't feel guilty for wanting to achieve your best. Go for gold – you have the energy, confidence and charisma to handle any situation.

FAMILY, FRIENDS AND HOME LIFE

There are some people who may seem generous and kind on the surface, but are their motives pure or do they have hidden agendas? Promise yourself to look again, because not everything you see before you is the truth.

Hecate

Tradition: Ancient Greek
Symbols: serpent, black dog, crossroads, flaming torch, key
Lunar cycle: dark of the moon in Libra
Sacred crystals: moonstone, labradorite
Keywords: liminality, opportunity, choice

Key

Choice.

Oracle

You may be at a crossroads, but now is the time to take the next step on your journey. Hecate hands you a torch to light your way, but the path you take is your choice alone.

Myth

Originally believed to be a Thracian goddess, in Greek mythology Hecate was the daughter of the Titans Perses and Asteria. She was often depicted as a triple-headed goddess, but most often considered to be the crone aspect of the triad of mother, maiden, crone, with Demeter as the mother and Persephone as the maiden. Hecate is also said to look to the past, present and future, and was known as the Queen of the Witches, accompanied by wild black dogs, serpents, cats and burning torches to light the way forward. With these torches, she helped the Earth goddess, Demeter, search for her daughter, Persephone. In some accounts, when Persephone was found as Hades's queen in the underworld, Hecate remained there with her as an older, wiser companion. Associated with crossroads, thresholds and sorcery, Hecate was revered for her knowledge of witchcraft and prophecy. She was worshipped during the Deipnon – a feast held to honour her entourage of restless spirits during the dark of the new moon phase – and small statues of Hecate were often placed at entrances to the home and at cross-roads to ward off evil.

Meaning and Wisdom

Hecate usually appears with her flaming torches at a time when you need to make a decision. Associated with liminal places, such as doorways and thresholds, Hecate represents the time between being faced with a decision and having to make the actual choice and aligns to the dark of the moon in Libra. Hecate roamed the underworld with the Lampades, her loyal torch-bearing nymphs, so shine a light on your own needs and desires. Ask yourself if what you need and what you want are at odds. What is it that you need to feel fulfilled? Making a choice is never easy, because we are letting go of a path not taken – and sometimes we may regret that choice. Hecate reminds you that there is no right or wrong and a choice you are faced with now is just one of many along the journey that is life.

Her Message

Hecate also rules boundaries, hedgerows, waysides and walls; similarly, she helps us to build personal boundaries. We don't have to build a fortress around us, but Hecate reminds us that we do at times need to know when to enforce our boundaries. Right now, consider your own limits. How far across the line will you let people go? Others may try to cast their own negativity on you, push you for answers, or claim you are responsible for their failings, but you can push back. Your boundaries are your choices; make it clear what those are.

To Invoke Hecate's Lunar Blessing

During the Deipnon celebration at the dark of the moon, offerings were made of root vegetables such as garlic, along with traditional libations of wine and cakes. Place a gift of a cake or wine on your altar with a candle, a key and an image of a black dog (Hecate's attributes). When you have done so, say, 'Hecate, help me to create choice boundaries,' and you will soon be blessed with her power.

Themed Oracles

ROMANTIC RELATIONSHIPS

Every day is filled with a myriad choices and when you look at relationships through the lens of Hecate, it's likely that you have a big decision to make. Do you commit, do you play it safe, do you ask for more, do you let go and move on? Whatever the question, Hecate implores you to stand at your personal threshold and look to the past and to the future, and then make the choice rather than stay in limbo. Do you want never to know, or live a life full of regret, of 'what ifs' and 'if onlys'? Step across the threshold, don't hold back or look back; any choice you make is always the right one.

LIFE PURPOSE

It is time to let go of something in your life in order to create something better. You may not be on the wrong track as such but finding it hard to take a leap of faith and trust your instincts. Be true to yourself and you will find yourself walking down the right road.

FAMILY, FRIENDS AND HOME LIFE

Breathe new life into an old project. What was once of no value may be worth more than you imagine. Dig deep into those mental drawers, or sort through your material possessions and you are sure to find something that needs to see the light of day.

Tārā

Key

Inner wisdom.

Oracle

**The pathway to contentment is open to you now, and
it is time to embrace self-belief, seek out your bliss and
discover new meaning in life.**

Myth

In most Buddhist iconography, Tārā is depicted as beautiful, playful
and always giving. Her origins are obscure, but she most likely
developed from the goddess Durga, of the ancient Vedic religion,

and was associated with the North Star – one of the principal stars for navigation for thousands of years. In Tibetan Buddhist tradition, one story suggests that Tārā was born from the tears of the compassionate *bodhisattva* (a person on the path to Buddhist enlightenment), Avalokiteśvara, when he wept on seeing the suffering of all beings in *saṃsāra* – the endless cycle of death and rebirth. His tears formed a pond and within the pond grew a lotus and Tārā arose from the flower. She is often depicted holding the *utpala* (blue lotus), which is said to be at its most fragrant at night, under the light of the moon.

Tārā has many emanations (twenty-one being the standard in most texts) that correspond to colours and associated qualities. For example, Red Tārā embodies power and transformation, while White Tārā, often seated on a white lotus, is concerned with healing, longevity and motherhood. As the female aspect of the universe, Green Tārā, who is considered the most important of her emanations, appears in another form as Tārā of the Acacia Forest, where she is associated with nature, forests, wild animals and the wind. Green Tārā embodies enlightenment and finding one's inner strength and conviction, and she also helps travellers to navigate successfully, whether along a physical or spiritual pathway.

Meaning and Wisdom

Tārā shines her light from the skies to remind you to look deep within the darkness of yourself to discover your own star. She tells you to seek that inner soul place where strength is found in times of trouble. Ask yourself, are you going through a difficult period in your life? Are you finding support outside of yourself, but have you yet to turn inwards and find your own metaphorical north star, hidden within? Reach inwards as well as out, just as the waning moon in Capricorn's energy influences us to realise that true integrity lies within us. Yes, look to the north star in the sky above you, and thank Tārā for her light, but see it also shining deep within you, always there to strengthen your resolve when you need it.

Her Message

If you feel lost in a tangled forest of feelings, a sea of turbulent emotions or a storm of uncertainty, Tārā assures you that the way forward is to find the north star, your inner compass, to point you in the right direction. And this north star is your own strength and purpose, a sense of integrity that comes from understanding how you can shine the best of your own starlight.

To Invoke Tara's Lunar Blessing

Look to the stars one clear night, and find the one that shines the brightest. Make a wish for future happiness and say, 'Thank you, Tārā, for looking down on me, now and for always. As I look to the stars in the sky and the moonlight in your eyes, I see my own light reflected back.'

Themed Oracles

ROMANTIC RELATIONSHIPS

Follow your heart, not your head. You already know the answer —
now dare to reveal it to yourself.

LIFE PURPOSE

Deep down, you know what you want for the future, yet there
always seems to be an obstacle of some kind to prevent you from
following that intuitive calling. With self-awareness and insight,
you can transform the roadblock in your head to a pathway to
freedom.

FAMILY, FRIENDS AND HOME LIFE

Home is where the soul is at peace. Now is the time to reach into
this soul place within yourself and find your inner comfort zone.

Rhiannon

Tradition: Celtic/Welsh
Symbols: white horse, singing birds, fertility, magic, shells, white candles, poetry
Lunar cycle: waxing moon in Libra
Sacred crystals: moonstone, clear quartz, bloodstone
Keywords: dignity, self-respect, composure, balance, harmony

Key

Compassion.

Oracle

Reach out to others with self-confidence and don't doubt yourself. You care about the world, so direct that care both inwards and outwards to nurture your heart and soul.

Myth

Often confused with the British horse goddess, Rīgantonā (meaning 'Great Queen'), or associated with the Gaulish horse goddess,

Epona, Rhiannon was immortalised in the *Mabinogion*, a collection of stories that was first documented in the eleventh century and an example of some of the earliest known British/Welsh prose literature.

In one myth, Rhiannon, a goddess from the Otherworld (the Celtic realm of the dead), married Pwyll, the prince of Dyfed (West Wales). When their newborn son, Pryderi, was mysteriously abducted, Rhiannon was wrongly accused of devouring her child. Her punishment was to sit beside the castle gatehouse every day, telling each traveller who passed through about her terrible crime and offering to carry them on her back up the hill to the castle like a horse. The newborn child had been snatched from its cradle by a monster and abandoned on the doorstep of the horse lord, Teyron of Gwent. Teyron and his wife took care of the child, who inherited the supernatural powers of his mother and grew to be a golden-haired young adult in seven years. Teyron, who had once been Pwyll's courtier, realised that the boy now resembled Pwyll, and nobly returned him to Dyfed. As soon as Pryderi was reunited with his mother, Rhiannon's punishment was ended.

Birds, horses, the wind, magic and poetry are sacred to the Welsh moon goddess who was said to have been born during the first-ever moonrise. She manifests as a beautiful woman riding a white stallion, surrounded by singing larks and occasionally birds of prey. As an archetypal figure of grace and generosity, composure and acceptance, Rhiannon encourages self-respect, dignity and compassion on those who invoke her power.

Meaning and Wisdom

Rhiannon represents not only compassion, but balance and impartiality, aligning to the waxing moon in Libra. She tells us to be generous but not give too much away; to play fair, but not to compromise just for the sake of keeping the peace. She is a goddess who reminds us that in the face of others' spite, reproach or accusation, if we can remain dignified and act with integrity, our truth will one day be revealed and respected. But even so, we must always respect ourselves first – for if we neglect our own interests, how can we experience true empathy for others?

Her Message

Have you been pleasing others instead of pleasing yourself? Are you the people-pleaser who always says 'yes', but never puts your own needs first? Rhiannon encourages you to learn to say 'no'. Learn to take a breath before you speak and then say, 'Sorry, I can't do that right now,' or 'Let me think about it,' without feeling you've let someone down or that maybe they'll stop liking you. In fact, Rhiannon asks, from where does this need to please others originate?

Rhiannon also prompts us to consider whether we have ever felt wronged, doubted our own judgement or felt compelled to remain calm and compromise. Because it's time to be true to who we really are. Rhiannon believes that loyalty and compassion are treasured qualities indeed – especially in difficult circumstances – but it's important that we are loyal and true to ourselves first.

Invoke Rhiannon's Lunar Blessing

To call on Rhiannon's power and encourage more compassion for yourself, invoke her power with this blessing. You may want to light a white tea-light candle when doing so:

> *By the glow of the moon, I see more clearly.*
> *Rhiannon, your flame now shines so fearlessly.*
> *As I look up to the skies tonight,*
> *I will find my soul, my own true light.*

Now, close your eyes, relax, and imagine you are Rhiannon, riding a white horse through the cosmos. As you take hold of the reins, you are no longer burdened by the weight of other people's demands or problems, nor those who are 'riding on your back', taking advantage of your good nature. Immerse yourself in this sense of freedom and acknowledge your worries being dispersed into the universe.

Themed Oracles

ROMANTIC RELATIONSHIPS

You now have the gift of freedom to choose what you want from a relationship. Is it a future commitment, or a realisation that you need more space to do your own thing? If you're looking for love, open your heart and soul to future possibilities and be patient. The one you need will come to you soon.

LIFE PURPOSE

Don't doubt your talents, show them off. Rhiannon reminds you that if you have a strong feeling to go in a certain direction, do so, but you also need to be proactive, make new connections and not just leap in at the deep end. Wait one lunar cycle from now before you commit, to ensure you make the right choice. Don't let self-doubt ruin your long-term goals or plans.

FAMILY, FRIENDS AND HOME LIFE

You are currently looking for harmony in your life, but don't want to upset others by putting your own needs first. Yet Rhiannon urges you not to fear speaking up, as it's time to be an ambassador for yourself. With a logical and civilised approach, you can make it clear what has to change and how.

Brigid

Tradition: Irish/Celtic
Symbols: cow, St Brigid's Cross, serpent, fire, poetry, wells
Lunar cycle: full moon in Leo
Sacred crystals: sunstone, red jasper
Keywords: creative inspiration, motivation, stimulation, excitement

Key

Creativity.

Oracle

From the depths of a sacred well, a fire arises in its secret water. Likewise, draw on your creative source, for it lies within your deepest self if you dare to look.

Myth

Brigid, also known as Bride, Brigit and Bridget, is the Celtic goddess of creativity, wisdom, sacred wells, springs and poetry, and in some accounts, the moon and the sun. She was also goddess of springtime, fire, and the flames of inspiration and healing.

In Irish mythology, Brigid was the daughter of the powerful god, Dagda, the father of a race of supernatural people known as Tuatha Dé Danann. Her sacred animals include the serpent, wolf, cow and various birds of prey. Assimilated into Christianity as the Irish patroness (mother) saint of healing and protection of the home, Saint Brigid's convent in Kildare was believed to have been built on the original site of a pagan shrine to the earlier goddess, Brigid. Even as a nunnery, it was still renowned for its supernatural powers, where flowers sprung up in the saint's footprints, cows were always in milk and it was eternally springtime in the convent garden. In the twelfth century CE, the historian Gerald of Wales wrote that nineteen nuns (the earlier goddess's priestesses) took turns to keep a sacred fire burning in Brigid's honour after her death on 1 February in either 524 or 525 CE, which coincides with the traditional day of the pagan festival of Imbolc. According to Gerald, the fire was encircled by a hedge and any man who tried to cross it would be cursed, and it is believed that on the twentieth day of the month, Saint Brigid herself appeared to tend the fire.

The St Brigid's Cross (her most popular symbol as Catholic saint) was made from rushes and is an off-centre cross woven around a central square. In pagan tradition, it symbolises the four seasons and four elements (fire, earth, air and water) and was traditionally hung over doorways to protect the home. Brigid's other pagan motif, the Bride Doll, represents feminine wisdom, inspiration and creativity and was placed in the home to encourage fertility and blessings.

Meaning and Wisdom

The goddess Brigid comes into your life to awaken you to your own inner fire: the fire of inspiration, creativity and a sense that you are in touch with the gods. The great bards of medieval Ireland truly believed that their inspiration came from divine sources, and similarly, Brigid says it's time to ignite your own creative flame. The word 'inspire' is rooted in a Latin word for 'breath' – *inspirare* – and for many people inspiration is the breath of creative life. The nineteen high priestesses who eternally tended Brigid's fire remind us that to feel blessed and nurtured, we need to constantly stoke our own spark of life, the fire of inspiration within, for without it we become dull, tainted, regretful or negative.

Her Message

Welcome Brigid into your life by focusing on the positive. Discover within you a new talent or reinvent an old one, or dig deep to find what might give you meaning or a sense of stimulation and fulfilment. The full moon in Leo is a time of breakthrough, creative power and fulfilment, so Brigid is here to fan your own inspirational flame. Perhaps you are currently lacking motivation, courage or even physical or mental energy? Brigid reminds you that this is the time to open your mind and heart to being inspired by the world around you, and you will soon have a clearer picture of your own creative potential and what to do with it.

To Invoke Brigid's Lunar Blessing

Brigid's sacred number is nineteen, associated with the nineteen priestesses who tended her fire. To call on Brigid to bring you creative inspiration, safely light a white tea-light candle and let the flame burn for nineteen minutes before extinguishing it. As you blow or snuff it out, say, 'Come to me now, Brigid, and bring me the spark of inspiration. Thank you for my gift of creativity, blessed be.'

Themed Oracles

ROMANTIC RELATIONSHIPS

Be spontaneous, take a leap of faith and trust in love and bring it to life. See love flourish rather than let the flames die down. Rekindling a relationship will bring you the happiness you seek.

LIFE PURPOSE

Unleash your creative power and manifest a current goal. Even if it looks like a long, hard road to realisation, this is an auspicious time to fire your metaphorical arrows high in the sky, knowing that when they come back down to Earth they will hit the right targets.

FAMILY, FRIENDS AND HOME LIFE

Now is the opportune time to bring new energy into the home, or among friends or family. Imagine your desired outcome, see clearly how it will all work out, and you will succeed. Trust in your vision, your innovative ideas and let inspiration be your guide.

Triple Goddess

Tradition: Celtic, Hindu, Greek, Roman, Norse and others
Symbols: crescent, full and waning moon, silver
Lunar cycle: full moon in Capricorn
Sacred crystals: moonstone, clear quartz crystal, black tourmaline
Keywords: meaning in life, value, self-discovery and cosmic connection

Key

Significance.

Oracle

Focus on how far you have come right now, not on how far you have yet to go. The present is a gift, so live for the moment.

Myth

In many mythological traditions around the world, some form of the triple goddess (three goddesses in one) has been revered and worshipped, such as the triple aspect of Hecate (see page 57), the Fates, the Graces, The Morrígan and the Horae (goddesses of the seasons), all of whom represent the three main phases of the moon – waxing, full and waning – and likewise, three aspects of womanhood – maiden, mother and crone. The Tridevi is a Hindu trinity of goddesses, made up of Saraswati, Lakshmi and Parvati. Many sources believe that all these triple goddesses represent three aspects of the archetypal Great Goddess, thought to have been worshipped in Neolithic times long before patriarchal civilisation. As such, the Great Goddess has appeared in many guises and many aspects around the world. She is often associated with archetypal Mother Earth goddesses, such as Cybele and Gaia of Greek myths, Mahadevi, the supreme goddess in Hindu myth, and the Roman Magna Dea.

The symbolism and worship of the triple goddess have been adopted by many neopagan belief systems, including Wicca. In Wicca, the maiden represents the crescent waxing moon, enchantment, new beginnings, youth, creativity, innocence and springtime. The mother represents the full moon, ripeness, fertility, sexuality, fulfilment and summer. The crone represents the waning moon, wisdom, repose, endings, relinquishment and autumn and winter.

Meaning and Wisdom

Whatever her ancient origins, the triple goddess comes into your life to remind you to look at what motivates you, what is significant in your life and what you hope to achieve as you align with the different cycles of the moon. The triple goddess aligns with the full moon in Capricorn, where traditional values are upheld and the present is considered to be a gift, but she asks you to consider all lunar phases as a whole. During the full moon, complete projects, fulfil plans and dance under the moonlight to give thanks to the universe. Feel connected to the waxing moon and use that time to get inspired and creative. Respect the waning or dark of the moon as a time to put down tools, to restore your energy with rest, repose, reflection and renewal. The triple goddess also tells you that the more you are conscious of all the lunar phases and how you relate to them, the more you are becoming aligned to her power and the embodiment of the cosmos itself.

Her Message

The triple goddess dances into your life to remind you that she permeates all. This divine feminine source lies within you and if you can develop your spiritual awareness, the triple goddess will bring you great joy, comfort, happiness and a sense of significance. Realise you have a sacred self and take time for self-reflection and meditation. Find moments of serenity and silence, take a walk in nature, gaze up to the skies or the stars, and you will feel at one with not only yourself, but the goddess in all her aspects as she changes with the lunar cycles. The triple goddess asks you to consider what gives you meaning in life, what feels significant and what truly matters most to you. When you know the answers to these questions, you know yourself.

To Invoke the Triple Goddess's Lunar Blessing

Light a tea-light candle in honour of the triple goddess and gaze into the flame for a few moments. Reflect on her as goddess of spring and the waxing moon, then imagine her as goddess of summer and the full moon, then finally, goddess of autumn, winter and the waning moon. Symbolically, you are aligning your own spiritual self with these lunar cycles, and if you continue to perform this simple ritual at each phase of the moon, you will soon feel her all-encompassing power enriching your life.

Themed Oracles

ROMANTIC RELATIONSHIPS

You are realising the significance of one special relationship and, although a beautiful feeling, it comes with its own set of risks and choices. But at the heart of the matter is knowing what you value most in life right now and aligning with that value. This is the choice you need to make.

LIFE PURPOSE

Very soon you will know who you are and where you are going. Although you may still look back, look at yourself in the here and now. It is only by self-belief and the discovery of who you are that you can have the life that you desire.

FAMILY, FRIENDS AND HOME LIFE

Achievement is a personal objective and during this time you know there is something you must do for you and you alone. Don't fear repercussions and sticking up for yourself, go with the flow and things will improve for the better.

Nimue

Tradition: Arthurian/Celtic
Symbols: lake, sword, hawthorn tree, may blossom
Lunar cycle: waning moon in Pisces
Sacred crystal: clear quartz, amethyst
Keywords: beguilement, seduction, self-deception, idealism

Key

Seduction.

Oracle

Don't deceive yourself about what you truly want and need right now. Act upon what you know to be real, rather than being led astray by your ideals and fantasies.

Myth

Nimue is usually associated with the Lady of the Lake, the iconic figure of Arthurian legend. For the purposes of this book, I refer to the Nimue as described in Thomas Malory's fifteenth-century *Le*

Morte D'Arthur. In this story, she is compassionate but determined, shrewd yet sensible, enchanting and powerful.

When King Arthur's magician and adviser, Merlin, fell in love with the enchantress, Nimue, he became obsessed with her beauty and charm. But his infatuation for Nimue made her feel trapped, both sexually and emotionally. Unable to free herself from his clutches, but having gained all his magical knowledge, she sealed him in a hawthorn tree, or in some accounts in a crystal cave, so he could no longer pursue her. She then became Arthur's magician and trusted adviser.

In one story, Nimue saves Arthur from the sorceress Morgan Le Fay's attempt on his life and from death at the hands of Morgan's lover, Accolon. In Malory's tale, Nimue eventually becomes the lover of Pelleas, a gentle knight whom she protects with her magic. After Arthur's final battle, Nimue is one of the enchantress queens who arrive in a black barge to bear the mortally wounded Arthur to his eternal resting place at Avalon.

Meaning and Wisdom

Nimue's story reminds us that being seen as seductive is both a blessing and a curse. It can seem like a gift when we appear to have the power to beguile someone romantically. With that power, we feel good about ourselves. We may do this totally unconsciously or we may act this way because of the interaction with the other person. The curse is that we may unconsciously repeat seductive roles to feed our self-worth, or always be attracted to seductive types and then get let down. Nimue comes to tell us that seduction is a quality that, like love, permeates our psyche in many different forms. The waning moon in Pisces reflects bewitching behaviour, both in the way that we can be led astray by our own ideals and how we made lead others astray from their pathway too.

Her Message

Nimue comes to ask you if you have recently been infatuated with an idea or a person and if so, how did it make you feel? She tells you not to let yourself be led astray by your dreams or deceive yourself about others. When we want to achieve a task, or find out information, we often smile and put on the charm, because to be seductive gives us self-confidence. We all tease, tempt, smile sweetly or do what's necessary to have our wants and needs met. Nimue says take care, don't go too far. You need to be totally honest with yourself about your intentions.

To Invoke Nimue's Lunar Blessing

To ensure Nimue leads you to understand who you really are and what you want, hold a white quartz crystal close to your belly for a few moments and say, 'Nimue, thank you for leading me to know myself and to see through self-deception and illusion.'

Themed Oracles

ROMANTIC RELATIONSHIPS

Don't be fooled by the words of another, or even your own illusions. Right now, you need a discerning eye to penetrate the truth of a relationship. It is time to act, as long as it's with clarity and insight.

LIFE PURPOSE

You may have been misled by circumstances not in your control, or haven't really looked to the future with clarity. But you're beginning to see through the fog and can start to see the light of reason.

FAMILY, FRIENDS AND HOME LIFE

Being an empath has its downside right now, so cultivate a protective aura around you so you have a chance to think your own thoughts and not feel led astray by other people's problems. You need space to be yourself.

Lilith

Tradition: Sumerian/Babylonian
Symbols: owl, serpent, poppies, frankincense
Lunar cycle: dark of the moon in Sagittarius
Sacred crystals: black moonstone, obsidian, black agate
Keywords: sexual power, desire, dissension, confrontation

Key

Defiance.

Oracle

Stand up for your beliefs, your identity and your true self. Listen to what comes from your soul and let Lilith's words of freedom liberate you from your darkest night.

Myth

Originally an ancient Sumerian or Babylonian goddess, Lilith has moved through mythological history with the defiant nature of a free spirit: wild, passionate and untameable. She is said to be a handmaiden to the goddess Inanna (see page 135), guiding followers to Inanna's sacred temple for sexual rites. Lilith is often identified as Adam's first wife, before Eve, who refused to have sex with him in the submissive missionary position. Rather than become a subject of patriarchal will, Lilith chose exile and left Eden. She was then identified as a demon succubus in Hebrew mythology and by the nineteenth century had become associated with the archetypal femme fatale. Her role as a dark of the moon goddess aligns with this lunar phase in Sagittarius, a time of wild spirits, satyrs and nymphs dancing in the dark as they cast their magical power wildly, passionately and freely.

Artists and writers have long been influenced by Lilith's defiant, liberated femininity. Pre-Raphaelite artist Dante Gabriel Rossetti first painted a version of *Lady Lilith* in 1862 with Fanny Cornforth as the model. But in 1872, he replaced Fanny's face with Alexa Wilding, a woman who to Rossetti represented the revival of feminine power, her hair an erotic symbol in his archetypal modern Lilith. Rosetti's accompanying sonnet inspired later pre-Raphaelite John Collier to paint another well-known version of Lilith, where she is depicted with a serpent coiled around her, as if in ecstasy from its embrace.

Meaning and Wisdom

Lilith comes into your life to ask you to reclaim your power – both sexual and personal – and stand up for who you truly are. Is there someone who is trying to undermine you or curtail your freedom in some way? Are you being asked to lie, metaphorically, in the missionary position? Lilith reminds you that equality is also about accepting others' need to feel equal and to consider your impact on those around you. Lilith asks you to check in with yourself and ask if you are truly as liberated as you want to be. Accepting and understanding your own level of power is the key to taking control of your life.

Her Message

As handmaiden to Inanna, Lilith encourages you to enjoy your sexuality, to embrace your sexual needs and to free yourself from preconceived notions of how you should behave, as long as you are causing no harm. Taboo subjects come under Lilith's domain, but she reminds us that whatever we believe, or think is right for us, may not be for others. Yes, be defiant and show your individuality and true desires, but accept others' individuality too. Lilith may have been dangerously divine and repressed by patriarchal civilisations, but she carries the sacredness of safeguarding one's sexual identity. She asks you to consider: what are my sexual needs and how do I honour and fulfil them? Lilith's message is to show not only a little defiance, but to stand up for your beliefs. Don't deny yourself your needs, defy the expectations of others.

To Invoke Lilith's Lunar Blessing

Lilith represents the power within us that can never be taken away, regardless of what's happening around us. On the surface, we may feel overwhelmed or vulnerable, yet if we dig deep into our psyche during the dark of the moon, we will discover the spark of our own power. Look into a mirror, and look deep within your eyes to your soul, and you will glimpse the power that needs to come to the light. Like the dark invisible moon that will become an empowering new crescent moon in the days to come, Lilith reawakens your power. All you have to do is ask.

Themed Oracles

ROMANTIC RELATIONSHIPS

Stay strong and positive if you are going through a tricky phase with someone and use your strength and self-belief to see yourself through. You may have to go against someone else's opinion, but courage is needed to say your piece and in that revelation, you know that you are being honest with them, but most of all with yourself.

LIFE PURPOSE

This may be a time of uncertainty about your abilities, or you are being challenged or provoked into planning a future you don't truly desire. Reject self-doubt or others who try to push you in one direction when you know in your heart what is true for you. The power is now in your hands; decide how to use it wisely to invest in your future.

FAMILY, FRIENDS AND HOME LIFE

Be bold in your choices but remain open-minded and listen to your family or friends. You may currently be involved in a lot of organising and this means you can feel resentful that you can't have more time to yourself. With all the conflicting demands on your time, see that you are still achieving positive results and that sometimes, a little patience is a refreshingly new way to rebel.

Arianrhod

Tradition: Celtic/Welsh
Symbols: silver wheel, Corona Borealis, castle, sea, loom
Lunar cycle: full moon in Aquarius
Sacred crystals: amber, abalone shell, haematite
Keywords: unconventional, free-spirited, contrary, open-minded

Key

Independence.

Oracle

As the silver wheel turns, take a leap of self-belief and an opportunity will appear. Diversify and be different, don't deny yourself the chance to take an unfamiliar pathway to happiness.

Myth

In Welsh tradition, Arianrhod was the enchantress sister of the trickster, Gwydion. By most accounts, her name, meaning 'silver wheel', refers either to her identification with the full moon's silver light in the dark night, or her association with spinning and weaving – in many tales she was said to thread magic spells on her silver loom. In the traditional Welsh literature known as the *Mabinogion*, Arianrhod is central to the legend of Math, the king of Gwynedd. An ancient curse foretold that unless he was at war, Math had to rest his feet in the lap of a virgin, otherwise he would die. The trickster Gwydion suggested his sister, Arianrhod, to be Math's foot bearer, but she was not a virgin, and when she 'stepped over Math's wand' (a possible euphemism for having sex with him to prove she was a virgin), she instantly gave birth to Llew. In horror, Math banished her from court and Gwydion adopted Llew. Because Gwydion had tricked her, Arianrhod put three curses on Llew. The first, refusing to name him; the second, denying him the right to warrior's armour and third, refusing him a mortal wife. But with the more powerful wiles of Gwydion, Llew was released from all three curses and eventually was married to the flower maiden, Blodeuwedd (see page 123).

The banished Arianrhod was thought to live in a castle in the sky (or some accounts say the castle was hidden under the sea) known as Caer Arianrhod. She was said to have lived a lascivious life, gallivanting with spirits and casting wondrous spells. Her silver wheel carried dead warriors to her starry palace, which was also thought to be a portal between worlds, and it was here that she ruled, an outcast perhaps, but independent; a lady of the stars and of the deep sea, submerged, but also above reproach.

Meaning and Wisdom

How can this seemingly uncaring mother help you? We must see Arianrhod's banes as challenges that force us to grow and pursue new opportunities, rather than sitting in limbo all our lives. Arianrhod isn't perfect, nor does she care about conforming to the rules. She is free-spirited, staunchly independent and able to see beyond what society or convention expects. This reflects the phase of the full moon in Aquarius, when the spirit of rebellion overrides that which is apparently 'right' for us. Arianrhod lives in a liminal place, a curious mixture of the submerged palace and the heavenly one, preferring neither, her silver wheel turning between worlds to offer an unusual perspective on life. It is often in such a transitional place that we can see other, more diverse possibilities that are available to us.

Her Message

In this moment of liminality, Arianrhod has come into your life to help you see all the potential paths open to you and to remind you that you alone have the responsibility for making choices. The moment you realise this is Arianrhod's moment. Yes, turn the silver wheel and see life from a different perspective. Look outwards for opportunity and look within for your own unique talent. You are blessed with unfulfilled potential, so don't bend to anyone's expectations. Remain independent and follow your bliss.

To Invoke Arianrhod's Lunar Blessing

Gaze for a few moments at yourself in a mirror and say:

> *I am both light and shade, I am both night and day, I am both full moon and dark of the moon. Here, with balance and poise, grace and acceptance, I am myself. If I see my potential and delight in my independent spirit, then I am free to make my own choices too. Thank you, Arianrhod, for your blessing.*

Themed Oracles

ROMANTIC RELATIONSHIPS

It is time to realise that someone is having trouble understanding who you really are. They may have blinded themselves with their own illusion of what they wanted you to be, so now is the time to defend your purpose and your independence. It is your right.

LIFE PURPOSE

Being swayed in several directions by those who think they know better than you isn't exactly helping you to make a choice. You know your abilities, you know your skills and you know where you truly want to be. Just be it.

FAMILY, FRIENDS AND HOME LIFE

Whatever happens now, keep your wits about you and realise that a personal family mission has been accomplished. As a result of your efforts, you now have a greater sense of independence too. Don't fear your growth in self-reliance, be fearless and enjoy standing out from the crowd.

The Vile

Key

Clarity.

Oracle

Don't be blind to the truth, nor blind yourself to what that might be. Only you know the answer and if it means changing your mind, then dare to do so.

Myth

In Slavic folklore, a vila (plural: vile) was a woodland, mountain, water, cloud or nature spirit, who in some stories was likened to a hunter with a bow and arrow, or a warrior similar to the Valkyries of Norse mythology. These nature spirits were described as being incredibly beautiful, with the whitest of skin, their long white hair exuding magical power. The vila could shapeshift into any form – such as a swan, wolf, snake or bird – and even become the wind or sprout wings as she drifted towards the moon. If provoked or slighted, a vila would seek vengeance upon those who wronged her. In some tales she blinded people, in others she healed those who had already been blinded, restoring their sight. Some folk tales tell how the vile danced together in circles beneath the stars and moon to seduce and lure mortals to their doom. As they were spirits of the indigenous forest, the fir tree was sacred to them. In most mythologies, they were the supernatural, all-seeing, all-knowing eyes who helped warriors on the battlefield by revealing an individual's fate and future.

Meaning and Wisdom

A vila is ambiguous and ever-changing. She keeps us guessing, never sure if she's on our side or about to blind us for a human failing. Yet her all-seeing, all-knowing power can bring us help and comfort when we're trying to resolve our own battles. She reminds us to connect to our intuition or to unleash our own inner spirit and rather than hesitate or prevaricate, let our own supernatural power guide us to the next stage of our personal journey. She is a wise shapeshifter and, likewise, if we can transform our negativity into positivity, if we can accept that we often blind ourselves to the reality of a situation, look the other way or are unwilling to see the truth, then we will see more clearly how we can live our lives with joy.

Their Message

The vile come to awaken you and open your spiritual eyes, the third eye, the intuitive eye, whatever you prefer to call it, and ask you to 'see' life not through the tangible or the earthly physical lens, but the supernatural way. When the moon is waxing in Aquarius, we can visualise other ways of communicating, living and being. So, the vile remind you to see beyond the veil of illusion, or at least become aware of this 'other realm', and you will discover such clarity of vision lies within you too. Once you have seen what you cannot see with just your eyes, it's possible to view life and the world around you in an extraordinary way. The vile are omniscient, but don't expect you to be all-knowing; they waft down from the moon and the clouds to guide you to wake up to the spiritual, soulful 'eye' within.

To Invoke the Vile's Lunar Blessing

The vile ask you to open your spiritual eyes. First, close your eyes, place your thumbs over your closed lids and make a triangle by connecting your index fingers on your forehead. Stay like this for a few minutes. Relax and imagine you have only one eye, let's call it your third eye, in the centre of this triangle. Speak to the vile as you imagine 'seeing' them with this spiritual eye:

I see you clearly now, and with this sight restored I see all that I could not see before.

When you feel intuitively ready, open your eyes and thank the vile for giving you another viewpoint. Use this ritual whenever you need to 'see' a deeper truth.

Themed Oracles

ROMANTIC RELATIONSHIPS

Deep down you know what you truly want, and intuitively you are beginning to see how to solve a difficult problem. Yet you still don't have the courage to reveal your thoughts. Now is the time to speak up, trust in your inner voice, and follow through with action.

LIFE PURPOSE

Making it clear how ambitious or determined you are to succeed in your plans is one thing, but it's also important to look clearly at what you may be giving up in the process.

FAMILY, FRIENDS AND HOME LIFE

Looking logically at all the options of a new project is fine on the surface, but for everyone's peace of mind it's better to trust your inner voice at this particular time.

Isis

Tradition: Egyptian
Symbols: *tyet* knot, myrrh, wings, cow, hawk, silver
Lunar cycle: waxing moon in Scorpio
Sacred crystals: clear quartz, bloodstone, red carnelian
Keywords: wholeness, boundlessness, fulfilment, integrity

Key

Conviction.

Oracle

I am all that I am, and I am you. In this, you are boundless, heartfelt, whole; and I, this oracle, tell you that destiny is all your own.

Myth

As one of the most revered deities in ancient Egypt, Isis was the goddess of enchantment, sorcery, magic, healing, protection, motherhood, fertility, sky, moon, rain and the cosmos. She was the consort to Osiris, god of fertility, the afterlife and resurrection, who was killed and dismembered by her brother Set. After killing Osiris, Set scattered his body across the lands and Isis found all of the pieces except Osiris's penis. She reassembled his body and through magic and healing, brought him back to life. Some say she replaced his penis with a gold replica so that they could then go on to conceive the sun god Horus.

The worship of Isis spread across the Mediterranean with Alexander the Great's conquests in the late 4th century BCE, resulting in the conflation of culture and tradition throughout Ptolemaic Egypt and Greece. Isis, like the cult of Serapis, the god of Heaven and Earth, appealed to people from a variety of different cultures. To the Egyptians, she was the goddess of the moon and rain and was called the 'Nile in the Sky'. To the Greeks, she was associated with the lunar goddess Artemis. With Hellenistic culture absorbed into Rome in the first century BCE, the cult of Isis became part of Roman religion too. In this Greco-Roman world, the cult of Isis blossomed. First she was revered as a moon goddess to balance the solar power of Serapis and, as her cult developed, she also became the goddess of time, seasons and fertility of the earth. Isis was also the divine embodiment of a woman and in the Greco-Roman world she was usually depicted with cow's horns surrounding the full moon or, some say, a solar disc.

Meaning and Wisdom

Isis is a reminder that you can be made whole and nurtured to fulfilment, however broken or fragmented you may feel. This is the time to mother yourself, conceive a new you or revive a favoured lost version of yourself. The waxing moon in Scorpio is empowering and offers us determination and integrity. You may have lost track of your needs, your desires and your goals, but Isis encourages you to embrace the boundless sense of who you truly are and to give yourself the care you deserve. Do not neglect the way of truly being you; be the way you truly are.

Her Message

Ask yourself if you have recently felt as if you've been broken into fragments, emotionally or mentally. Who or what is putting pressure on you to be someone or something you're not? If you are at all unsure or feel fragmented, then Isis comes to give you the courage to restore a sense of wholeness and willpower, not just of the mind, but of inner heartfelt conviction and respect for yourself. She comes to tell you, 'Know that when things fall apart, they can fall together again.' If you feel confident and whole, then Isis's second gift of fulfilment is available to you to make choices and destiny all your own.

To Invoke Isis's Lunar Blessing

Place a red carnelian or bloodstone in a bowl of water and leave it outside during the night to draw down the moon's energy. The next day, remove the stone and keep it in your pocket or bag to enhance your connection to Isis and her nurturing, all-embracing power.

Themed Oracles

ROMANTIC RELATIONSHIPS

You may care deeply for someone right now, but don't become so involved that you repress your own emotional needs for the sake of theirs. Listen to their words deeply, let them speak freely, and with compassion and an open heart you will feel at one not only with them, but with yourself.

LIFE PURPOSE

Your pathway seems to be filled with obstacles, people who judge or criticise your methods or your choices, but it's your right to go your own way. Gather your strengths, drop your weaknesses and move on to better things. If someone says 'pull yourself together' they may have a point; in some way you have been pulled apart, but you now need to stand firm and be true to your convictions.

FAMILY, FRIENDS AND HOME LIFE

A kind relative or friend needs some emotional support and a tender-hearted acceptance of their uneasiness. You now have the chance to weave gentleness and kindness into your own life and by doing so, enhance mutual support for all.

Britomartis

Tradition: Greek
Symbols: fish, the sea, serpents, amaranth
  flower, axe
Lunar cycle: full moon in Virgo
Sacred crystals: citrine, peridot
Keywords: discerning, aloof, private, pure,
  composure

Key

Self-devotion.

Oracle

Envelop yourself in a cloak of poise and calm and the journey before you will no longer be filled with obstacles but with wisdom and wonder.

Myth

Originally a Minoan goddess of the hunt, fishermen and the moon, by most accounts Britomartis (meaning 'sweet maiden') was a virgin nymph who denied male suitors and was loved by the goddess Artemis. She was the daughter of Zeus and Carme (Carme's father, Eubuleus, was the son of the goddess of harvest, Demeter), and such was her beauty that Minos, king of Crete, fell in love with her and pursued her across his island for nine months. Her only means of escape was to leap from the cliffs into the sea, but she became entangled in a fishing net (she is also known as Diktynna, lady of the nets) and was saved by Artemis, who transformed her into a moon goddess. On the island of Aegina, her cult flourished and she was known there as Aphaia. Although she was a virgin goddess, Minoan archaeological statues show a darker side of her, as a hunter in the mountains accompanied by wild beasts, holding either a double axe or two divine serpents, representing her dual powers of wildness and purity. The Minoans believed she possessed a wild and darker nature, but this changed when she was assimilated into Greek culture and became associated with purity.

Meaning and Wisdom

Britomartis made it clear she wouldn't be pursued by men. She was only interested in worshipping Artemis and perhaps only being loved by her too. (She is often identified with Artemis's attributes and perhaps even conflated with her.) Britomartis is principled and steadfast in her own beliefs as demonstrated by her decision to plunge into the sea and face almost certain death, rather than become a victim of King Minos's lust. Even entangled in a fishing net, she managed to stay calm until she was saved by Artemis and immortalised as the moon. Britomartis reminds us of our own self-value. She asks, what are your values, what are your standards and how far will you let other people go before you make it clear what your limitations are?

Her Message

When Britomartis fell into the sea and was caught in the fishing net, she escaped her greatest fear. So, ask yourself, what would you escape from if you didn't know where that escape might take you – except perhaps away from the source of an emotional vulnerability? Britomartis reminds you to pay a little more devoted attention to yourself, reflecting the influence of the full moon in self-possessed Virgo; never to give all of yourself away or sacrifice your values for the sake of others. Once ensnared in the net of their expectations, you might lose yourself and your self-esteem forever.

To Invoke Britomartis's Lunar Blessing

Take any crystal of your choice, hold it tightly to your belly for a minute or so and close your eyes as you imagine being filled with light that is shining through you from the crystal, filling your whole body with the pure yet wild goodness of Britomartis. When you feel intuitively ready, open your eyes and place the crystal on a window ledge or an outside space to draw on the power of the moon overnight. The next day hold it close to you again and thank Britomartis for her gift of self-containment.

Themed Oracles

ROMANTIC RELATIONSHIPS

You want things to be flawless or uncomplicated, yet there seems to be something that keeps a relationship a little more tainted than you would like. Enter the net of self-enquiry and you'll discover what it is.

LIFE PURPOSE

Right now, you are radiating an aura of self-assurance and vitality. Use it to your benefit in all ambitious plans for the future, and if you want to change your mind about any long-term goal, now is the perfect moment to do so.

FAMILY, FRIENDS AND HOME LIFE

Some family want things to be clean, tidy and above board. Yet, for all your help and attention, you just don't seem to be getting it right in their eyes anyway. Don't strive for perfection any more, strive for tenacity and strength of mind.

Blodeuwedd

> **Tradition:** Welsh
> **Symbols:** owl, oak, broom, meadowsweet, spring
> **Lunar cycle:** dark of the moon in Aquarius
> **Sacred crystals:** onyx, obsidian, amber
> **Keywords:** self-respect, betrayal, truth, honesty

Key

Truth.

Oracle

Open your eyes to the truth, respect your inner wisdom and be honest about what you really want. If you are not true to your own desires, then you are betraying yourself – and if you betray yourself, you betray others.

Myth

In Welsh legend, Blodeuwedd was believed to be a spring and moon goddess, who may have originally been the consort of the Celtic sun god, Lugh. Aligning with the dark of the moon in Aquarius, a time when our sense of freedom is put to the test, or lies dormant, Blodeuwedd appeared as a central character in *The Mabinogion*, a body of medieval Welsh literature. Llew, was the son of the goddess Arianrhod (see page 99), who had put a curse on him so that he would never have a human wife. Llew wanted a wife desperately, so he asked his cousins Math and Gwydion, who were both magicians, to help. They created Blodeuwedd out of oak, meadowsweet, broom and various other spring flowers, but she was never happy with Llew and fell in love with the huntsman, Gronw. Desperate to be together, the couple conspired to kill the apparently invulnerable Llew. Blodeuwedd asked Llew to show her the only way he could be harmed. He trusted and loved her and it didn't cross his mind she wanted him dead. But Blodeuwedd betrayed him, allowing Gronw to stab Llew to death. With the fatal blow, Llew instantly transformed into an eagle that flew away, only to return months later and punish the lovers for their betrayal. Gronw was killed and Blodeuwedd was transformed into an owl so she would never be seen again in daylight. (Blodeuwedd meaning 'flower face', is also a Welsh name for an owl).

Meaning and Wisdom

Although Blodeuwedd may have conspired to kill her husband, we see her actions as an attempt to break free from the stereotypical gender role of wife. If we are champions of female freedom, then we can see Blodeuwedd as bold and fearless in her desire to free herself from a husband she had not chosen for herself and whom she had never loved, to be with someone she did. This also aligns with the dark of the moon in Aquarius, when we often unconsciously want to escape an apparent restriction and discover a new truth.

It seems that the flower goddess stuck to her belief and, in her undoing, acquired the symbolic wisdom of the owl.

Her Message

There are many questions that Blodeuwedd comes to ask you, and it's time to find out the truth. Have you ever wronged someone or have you been wronged by another? Have you ever been swept away on a wave of passionate desire that's unstoppable, unforgettable, irresponsible? Have you ever been deceived by a lover? Blodeuwedd reminds you to open up and express your truth, for right now you also need to *hear* the truth – and mostly from yourself. Blodeuwedd asks you not to think of yourself as just a pretty 'flower face', but to immerse yourself in the counsel of the wise owl who sees the truth.

To Invoke Blodeuwedd's Lunar Blessing

To share your truth with yourself, write down what it is you want to admit. Then take a black crystal and place it on the paper. As you do, say: 'With truth revealed I am wiser now, and so I will no longer betray myself. Blodeuwedd, show me the way forward to self-respect and integrity and help me to understand my truth.' Keep the paper wrapped around the stone for one lunar cycle, then open it again to see if you have truly accepted this truth.

Themed Oracles

ROMANTIC RELATIONSHIPS

It's time to be honest with yourself about what you truly want. Have the courage to face the truth and soon you will feel ready to walk along the pathway of your choice.

LIFE PURPOSE

Don't give up on your quest even if someone else tells you otherwise. They may not have your best interests at heart; it's only you who knows what that is.

FAMILY, FRIENDS AND HOME LIFE

So much of our social life is spent unravelling secrets, betrayals or even the wrong choices that have been made. Whatever is not being said right now is probably best left unsaid. You will uncover more by pretending disinterest than by dissent.

Pasiphaë

Tradition: Ancient Greek/Minoan
Symbols: bull, stream, herbs, bronze, sun, moon,
   oracles
Lunar cycle: waning moon in Aquarius
Sacred crystals: clear quartz, fluorite, haematite
Keywords: restoring self-worth, foresight, intention,
   individuality

Key

Self-Worth.

Oracle

Whatever you can do or believe you can do, begin.

Myth

Pasiphaë is best known as the mother of the Minotaur and queen of Crete, but she was also referred to as a goddess of sorcery. The daughter of the sun god, Helios, and the Oceanid nymph Perse, she conceived the Minotaur after mating with the Cretan Bull. Because her husband, King Minos, failed to sacrifice his prize bull to Poseidon as promised, Poseidon cursed Pasiphaë to fall in love with the bull. Under her curse she lusted after the bull, so she hid in a hollow cow built by the craftsman Daedalus (who also designed the labyrinth in which the bull was trapped), which she used for their copulation. Although her story is one of shame, Pasiphaë was worshipped as an oracular goddess at Thalamae on mainland Greece. The ancient geographer, Pausanias (c. 110-180 CE), wrote that her oracle was located near a clear stream, flanked by bronze statues of Helios and Pasiphaë – the latter he equated with the lunar goddess, Selene.

Meaning and Wisdom

Despite her humiliation derived from Poseidon's curse, Pasiphaë was hugely respected and admired as an oracular goddess, as she was the daughter of Helios. Alongside him at her shrine, she shines as brightly as he does. Rather than being demoted to a cursed queen, she is elevated to a lunar deity with the power of prophecy. Pasiphaë comes into your life to show you that however much you may have surrendered to what seemed to be an inescapable infatuation or obsession, you still have the self-respect and dignity to rise above it all and restore self-worth.

Her Message

As an oracular goddess, Pasiphaë, like the waning moon in Aquarius, reminds you to look to the future and not to hang on to the past. To review and if necessary, revise your plans and intentions, and to see your virtues, talents and positive qualities as the key to your future happiness. With foresight, and without looking back, you can walk on the path to a truly inspiring future. Pasiphaë tells you to never give up on yourself and to see that there is always another day, another new lunar cycle through which you are beginning to express your true individuality.

To Invoke Pasiphaë's Lunar Blessing

Light a blue tea-light candle and gaze into the flame. See the flame as a light to your future, guiding you forward. As you snuff the candle, thank Pasiphaë for blessing you with self-worth.

Themed Oracles

ROMANTIC RELATIONSHIPS

It is time to let go of any regrets you have about a relationship. You may feel you've been a fool, humiliated or emotionally hurt, but whatever the cause of those feelings, there's no one to blame. Taking responsibility for your choices will offer closure.

LIFE PURPOSE

You can now move on to the place you want to be without anyone to hold you back. With grace and integrity, you are at a point where you can explore not only what is right for you, but also what is actually on offer.

FAMILY, FRIENDS AND HOME LIFE

Be realistic. Don't let impatient family or impulsive advisers tempt you to do something you might regret. Your future plans will unfold as you wish them to if you take a step back before you move forward.

Inanna

Tradition: Sumerian/Mesopotamian
Symbols: Venus, lion, eight-pointed star, wand, knot of reeds
Lunar cycle: dark of the moon in Leo
Sacred crystals: lapis lazuli, green aventurine, diamond
Keywords: renewal, survival, revival, restoration

Key

Soul-searching.

Oracle

When darkness comes, we long for the light. Now is the time to see both as one, just as a candle illuminated on a dark moon night reveals all.

Myth

The Sumerian goddess of the heavens during the Uruk period of 4,000 BCE to 3,100 BCE, Inanna (meaning 'Queen Moon' or 'Lady Moon') was the predecessor of the Mesopotamian goddess

Ishtar (see page 279), with whom she merged during the Akkadian period. She was later assimilated as the Greek goddess, Aphrodite. Associated with the planet Venus as both the morning and evening star, Innana was goddess of sexuality, the moon, fertility, rebirth and war. Her most well-known myth is the story of her descent to the underworld to visit her sister, Ereshkigal, its queen, to pay respect to her dead consort, Gugalanna. An earlier story suggests that Inanna was, in fact, responsible for the death of Gugalanna and when Ereshkigal discovered this during her visit, she struck Inanna dead and had her hung on a hook to rot. Enki, god of the Earth, negotiated Inanna's release from the underworld by offering Ereshkigal a substitute – Inanna's lover, the shepherd Damuzi, instead. Inanna returned to the upper world as the moon and Damuzi and his sister took her place in the underworld for six months each, to mark the two main seasons of the agricultural year.

Meaning and Wisdom

Most modern interpretations of Inanna's descent to the underworld are based on a Jungian metaphor that her story is a journey to meet one's own shadow, to see the dark side of oneself, embrace and own it, and thus be able to live life more authentically. Inanna reminds us that we all make mistakes and we can all cause harm to others without realising it. But taking responsibility for our actions and choices means we can redeem ourselves too. Inanna asks you, how ready are you to meet this dark side of yourself? The one that can make errors, feels anger, unintentionally cause emotional pain to others and yourself. The goddess says that even if you're hanging on a metaphorical hook of guilt and blame, you will grow stronger and be able to let go of self-recrimination. You have the opportunity to restore and revive, forgive yourself and others, and to free yourself of blame. So, are you off the hook, or still on it? Inanna managed to get off hers; this is a time to show you can too.

Her Message

Inanna's message is to forgive yourself for your faults and failings and to do a little soul-searching. After all, if you connect to the sacred part of yourself, there is no blame, no fault, no hidden agendas, all is One. So, it's time to reject self-sabotage, regret, negativity or fear. But it is a time to recognise that you are only human too.

This is also the influence of the dark of the moon in Leo, when we feel our 'centre-stage' status is being threatened in some way. Inanna nudges you with her lapis lazuli wand of restorative power, holds her knotted hook of reeds before you, and asks you to own your dark side. Once you reclaim your shadow, your sacred, wild and majestic self comes to life.

To Invoke Innana's Lunar Blessing

To align with Inanna's lunar power, take a lapis crystal and use it as a wand to draw a circle around you. Sit inside the circle for a few minutes and think of anything you would like to be forgiven for or anything you regret doing or saying. Don't overthink it, just let it be what it is, a thought. Then gently toss the crystal across the imaginary circle and you have now let go of that regret or negative thought. Stand up and, as you cross the line yourself, you have reclaimed your integrity with Inanna's blessing.

Themed Oracles

ROMANTIC RELATIONSHIPS

Is someone else's shadow looming over you or cutting out your light? Are you feeling confused, uncertain of your power? Time to delve deep and don't let past hurts, errors or bad judgements stop you from reviving your romantic spirit.

LIFE PURPOSE

If things are not working out as you want them to, reflect, revise and see that you can survive this time, all that you require is continued belief and resilience. You've been down in the dark places and you've come back to the light, but it seems there's a price to pay, perhaps a sacrifice, a change of heart or a new strategy to be the best of yourself. Whatever it takes, do it now – you are capable.

FAMILY, FRIENDS AND HOME LIFE

There is a sense of guilt among family or friends, but why are you feeling responsible for their regrets or silly deeds? Now is the time to show that you care and that you won't judge someone, even if you believe them to be in the wrong. The only right you can do is to support and stay impartial.

Chang'e

Tradition: Chinese
Symbols: silver, hare, rabbit, lantern
Lunar cycle: waxing moon in Pisces
Sacred crystals: jade, blue lace agate
Keywords: temptation, impulsiveness, naivety

Key

Impulsiveness.

Oracle

Some fantasies are best left as exactly that. Awaken to the truth before you are led astray by your imagination.

Myth

Chang'e (also known as Ch'ang O) was a beautiful Chinese moon goddess and the wife of the archer Hou Yi. In most accounts of her myth, she is led astray by her desire for eternal youth and immortality.

When long ago ten suns appeared in the sky, scorching the Earth until it was almost uninhabitable, the gods sent the skilled archer,

Hou Yi, to shoot down nine of the suns to save humanity. On the success of his mission, the gods rewarded Hou Yi with an elixir of immortality. Hou Yi was overjoyed with the gift and wanted to share it with Chang'e, but while he was out hunting, she found the elixir and drank it all without thinking of the consequences. Instantly, she began to float up towards the heavens and, realising her folly, went to hide on the moon. Hou Yi returned home, his wife gone and the elixir missing. When he discovered what had happened, he realised he could never join her and they were destined only to love one another from afar. To some, she is a graceful goddess who brings peace, prosperity and good fortune to those who honour her. But to others she is a lonely figure, eternally gazing down from her refuge, accompanied by her only friend, a jade rabbit, while she longs for the mortal life with Hou Yi that she sacrificed in a moment of weakness.

Meaning and Wisdom

In her desire to be eternally beautiful, Chang'e made a choice to drink the elixir without thinking of the consequences. She may have found refuge on the moon, but that escape was a high price to pay. As the waxing moon in Pisces is a time to be led astray by others, she reminds us that we can all be led astray by our own desires and must take care we don't live to regret that moment of choice. Perhaps we need to learn to see temptation for what it is, rather than be drawn towards an ideal without a realistic appraisal. Are you about to take an impulsive risk like Chang'e, or are you ready to step back and let go of the binding power of temptation? With a little caution and rational thought, you can objectively see the consequences of your actions. Emotional reaction isn't the answer now, but awareness of your motives is.

Her Message

We often long for something we don't have, even though we know that in the end, we might regret pursuing it. So, Chang'e tells you that this is your chance to see more clearly what enticement and temptation mean in your life. A little objectivity is needed right now, for although it might be a nice idea to escape to the moon, you might discover it has a dark side too. Let Chang'e instead empower you with her gentle regret, as — yes — sometimes it's worth following your dream, but don't trample on someone else's by not thinking everything through.

To Invoke Chang'e's Lunar Blessing

Draw a crescent waxing moon on a piece of paper. Above it, write three words that sum up a long-term goal. Fold the paper three times, then put it somewhere safe for one lunar cycle. If the goal you wrote has now changed, then you know Chang'e has helped you to see there is more than one possibility, but if the goal hasn't changed you can safely take the opportunity and follow your bliss.

Themed Oracles

ROMANTIC RELATIONSHIPS

If temptation comes out of the blue, don't let your emotions take over. Any commitment you make now is best done by standing back and taking an objective look at what you might win, and more importantly, what you might lose.

LIFE PURPOSE

Being excited about an idea, dream or new project will give you the energy to follow it through. Be aware of your limitations but use that knowledge to go beyond them to achieve your goal.

FAMILY, FRIENDS AND HOME LIFE

There are always people who will try to persuade you that their opinions are more valid than yours. Fall under their spell and you could lose sight of a possible goal.

Hina

Tradition: Polynesian
Symbols: seeds, birds, banyan tree, flowers, the sea
Lunar cycle: waxing moon in Virgo
Sacred crystals: pearl, black tourmaline, peridot
Keywords: peacemaker, reconciliation, intervention, negotiation

Key

Mediation.

Oracle

Moderation and conciliation are the keys to success. Negotiate and move forward.

Myth

Hina is known by many other names in the regions of Polynesia and the South Pacific, such as Hinatea (Fair Hina) and Hinauri (Dark Hina) or Māhina (moon), and as such there are numerous legends and stories about her. For the purposes of this oracle, she appears as the Tahitian lady of the moon.

One myth tells of Hina and her brother, Ru, who both loved to explore the seas. Alone on her canoe one evening, she saw the shimmering moon across the horizon and decided to visit it. She stepped off her canoe and onto the moon and decided to remain there forever, watching over travellers at night to ensure their safety, while Ru continued to circumnavigate the Earth as the sun.

The shadows on the moon were thought to be the branches of a great banyan tree beneath which Hina lived. She climbed the tree every day to remove bark to make clothes for the gods. One day, as she climbed higher up the tree, she broke off a branch which fell to Earth. From this branch, another tree grew and became the first banyan in the world. With its massive, table-like trunk, the tree became a ritual gathering place for discussion and mediation and was thought to be located in the village of Opoa, on the island of Ra'iātea in French Polynesia. Hina lived on the moon with an *u'upa* (a wild pigeon), who ate the figs from the tree. When a menacing *otaha* (man-of-war bird) tried to steal a bunch of ripe figs from the pigeon, Hina intervened and chased the predator away. She sent the pigeon down to Earth to drop the figs on the land, so that there would be banyan trees for all the people and all the birds.

Meaning and Wisdom

Hina reminds us how sharing our good fortune unconditionally leads us to peace and harmony. Equality is what matters to this lady of the moon. It is her ability to mediate, and to provide not only a sacred gathering place for people to discuss their worries, needs and preferences, but also to act as a peacemaker between the metaphorical predatory bird and the submissive one. Like the waxing moon in Virgo, Hina knows that through gentle negotiation and a desire for genuine peace, you too can enhance your own self-value. She shows you that you must sometimes intervene, or act as an intermediary, to restore harmony.

Her Message

We all have to learn to be more discerning, make impartial judgements, negotiate and reconcile our differences. Yet it's not only in relationships with others that we need to engage in mutually considered negotiations, but also in our relationship with ourselves. Hina asks us to look at how we reconcile our own conflicts, such as how we find a way to align an emotionally driven desire that is at odds with a practical outcome. Hina asks you to look at the options, to see where you can share and where you can give and take. The lady of the moon asks you to sit down with yourself across a metaphorical banyan-tree table and balance your desires with your needs. She also suggests you ask yourself which is more important to you right now, need or desire?

To Invoke Hina's Lunar Blessing

If you have the following crystals so much the better, but this blessing works with any black and white stones.

- 1 pearl or white shell (to represent the day)
- 1 black tourmaline crystal (to represent night)
- 1 black tea-light candle
- 1 white tea-light candle

Light the candles, place the pearl in front of the black candle, and the tourmaline in front of the white candle. Gaze into the candle flames in turn and say:

Hina, lady of the moon, fill me with your harmony, your understanding and wisdom of negotiation, so I can see that by day I will resolve to make peace with my darkness, and by night, know there is always the power of my own light to come.

Themed Oracles

ROMANTIC RELATIONSHIPS

You need to settle a disagreement or a dispute in a love relationship. Pleasing others is one thing, but unless you're pleasing yourself too, compromising behaviour isn't the answer. Hina tells you to restore peace by accepting your differences. 'I accept you for who you are and you accept me for who I am, your opinion matters to you and mine matters to me.'

LIFE PURPOSE

Some say, 'go that way', others say 'this way' – but the direction is not clear. Hina comes into your life to remind you to sit down and consider the pros and cons so that you can take an objective and enlightened view when it comes to making a decision.

FAMILY, FRIENDS AND HOME LIFE

You are asked to be a go-between to establish a happy medium in an ongoing family or social matter. Whether you find a solution you can put to others, or manage to arbitrate and smooth things over, your honesty and non-judgemental attitude is what is needed now.

Calypso

Tradition: Ancient Greek
Symbols: owl, falcon, the sea, cypress, aspen
Lunar cycle: waning moon in Libra
Sacred crystals: sapphire, rose quartz, citrine
Keywords: unconditional love, duty versus desire,
    altruism, letting go

Key

Letting go.

Oracle

**In setting someone free, we may become captive to our
own desire to repossess.**

Myth

The name Calypso translates as 'she who conceals'. The daughter
of Atlas, one of the Titans, and the nymph Pleione, Calypso was
a beautiful nymph who lived on the enchanted island of Ogygia.
When Odysseus washed up on her shore after a storm on his way
home from the Trojan War, Calypso healed his wounds and they

soon became lovers. Odysseus was torn between returning home to his wife, Penelope, and his love for the bewitching Calypso, who sang hypnotic songs among scented flowers and wove her loom with a golden shuttle. Calypso even offered to grant Odysseus immortality if he agreed to stay with her forever. According to Homer's *Odyssey*, she persuaded him to remain with her for seven years, but although Odysseus was captivated by Calypso, his mission was to return home to Ithaca, so the gods eventually intervened. Zeus sent Hermes to tell Calypso to let Odysseus go, so reluctantly she helped him to construct a raft and advised him on a safe route across the seas. When he finally set sail, she sadly waved goodbye with their two sons at her side. No one knows what then happened to Calypso.

Meaning and Wisdom

Calypso's myth reflects our personal struggles and how we may find ourselves caught between duty and desire or unconditional and conditional love. Although it was Odysseus who had been held captive by his love for Calypso, once he was freed the roles were reversed and ironically it was Calypso who was held prisoner to her grief and loss. Calypso chose to let him go, albeit reluctantly and under the pressure of the gods, because she realised it was Odysseus's duty to return home. Calypso reminds us that although we may yearn for what once was, when we unchain our heart and offer unconditional love, we can still love someone from afar.

Her Message

Calypso comes to remind you that if you have let go of something or someone that meant a lot to you, then it is still possible to hold on to precious and gentle memories. Can you truly give out unconditional love – that is, love someone with no expectations, no limitations, no conditions? Can you truly be compassionate and altruistic without asking for something in return? This is the challenge of the waning moon in Libra, when we may have to let go of the very things we love, but most importantly let go of our attachment to our loss. Maybe now is the moment to reflect on Calypso's kindness and consider how letting someone follow their own path, whether for duty or love of another, is also about relinquishing part of oneself, the part that clings to and feeds off that love. However much it hurts to let go, you will also discover that in accepting the pain, you can heal.

To Invoke Calypso's Lunar Blessing

Try this unbinding ritual to invoke Calypso's blessing, so she can help you to let go of the things or people that hold you captive.

Take a two-foot length of ribbon and tie three knots, one at each end and one in the middle. Find calm and stillness and then say, 'Calypso, now I untie the binds of love, to discover the freedom within myself.'

Untie the middle knot and then say, 'Untied, unbound, unpossessed.'

Untie the left-hand knot and then say, 'Free the first and then the last.'

Untie the last knot and say, 'The last is unbound, I am unwound.'

You will soon feel Calypso's unconditional love flowing through you.

Themed Oracles

ROMANTIC RELATIONSHIPS

Don't hang on to a relationship for fear of loss, for in that loss you will find a new departure and a new destination. The journey never ends, it's only just beginning.

LIFE PURPOSE

Are you willing to take a risk? This is the time to take a shot of courage and follow your instincts or intuition. The island you are on is lonely, but it will become even more remote and isolated if you don't take that symbolic raft and push off into the sea of opportunity.

FAMILY, FRIENDS AND HOME LIFE

There is someone in your clan who has made you feel you owe them something. But now is the time to set the record straight and show you have a right to live by your values and not by emotional blackmail.

Mélusine

Tradition: Northern European
Symbols: serpent, fish, streams, rivers, waterfalls, springs
Sacred crystals: peridot, jade, moss agate
Lunar phase: waning moon in Virgo
Keywords: self-nurture, compassion, reconciliation

Key

Forgiveness.

Oracle

Forgive yourself for any regrets or negative feelings you may have. Don't hold back on giving kindness and compassion to yourself, first and foremost.

Myth

This well-known medieval legend, with variations across Luxembourg, northern and western France and the Low Countries, is centred around Mélusine, a freshwater nymph. Mélusine was said to be the daughter of a beautiful fae known as

Pressine, and Elinas, the King of Albany (Scotland). Her name possibly derives from Mère Lusine, Mother of the Lusignans, connecting her to the French royal house that was powerful throughout Europe during the medieval period.

The best-known version of this legend was written by Jean D'Arras in 1392. When Elinas met the beautiful Pressine while out hunting, they instantly fell in love. But Pressine only agreed to marry the king if he swore never to watch her when she gave birth or bathed. Yet as she gave birth to triplet daughters, the king could not resist spying on her and broke his promise. Pressine fled with her daughters to the lost island of Avalon. When Mélusine was fifteen, she asked her mother why they never saw their father, so Pressine told the sisters about their father's betrayal. Enraged, Mélusine conspired with her sisters to destroy their father and, using their magical powers, they imprisoned him in a mountain.

When Pressine heard of their terrible deed, she incarcerated one daughter, Palatine, in the same mountain as Elinas, sealed another, Melior, in a gloomy castle and banished Mélusine forever, putting a curse on her so that she would take the form of a two-tailed serpent every Saturday. If any man should see her bathing on that day, she would then remain in serpent form forever. Mélusine made her home in the forests of western France, where one day, Count Raymondin of Poitiers wandered by. They fell in love but Mélusine told the count that if they were to marry, he must never watch her bathe on a Saturday and he had to respect her privacy. After many years of living a harmonious, enchanted life and having several children, the count's curiosity got the better of him and he saw Mélusine's serpent tails. He gasped in horror and Mélusine watched him run from the shadows. Instantly she was transformed into a serpent-tailed dragon and had no choice but to fly away. Yet, because she loved her children so much, she returned every night to feed and comfort them.

Meaning and Wisdom

How can we interpret Mélusine's story? How does it resonate with our own feeling world? For her rage at her father's betrayal and in her guilt for her revenge, she paid the price by being cursed. When she found love, the only way to keep it was for another promise to be kept. Then, with another oath broken, there was nothing she could do but take on her monstrous form and suffer. Yet she wouldn't let her own children suffer, for she felt undeniable maternal love. In the midst of all the betrayal, she remained loyal to her children. Similarly, the waning moon in Virgo's influence is self-forgiving, reconciling and caring.

Her Message

Mélusine comes into your life to remind you that forgiveness is needed now. However emotionally battered or hurt you may feel, however much you may self-sabotage or think you're not good enough, you need to forgive yourself for those feelings. There are no conditions here, you must be unconditional in your love for yourself. Show up for who you are and are becoming. Move on and restore your self-respect by giving yourself big hugs of caring love without blame, guilt or 'if onlys'. You are your own greatest gift.

To Invoke Mélusine's Lunar Blessing

Take a piece of peridot or moss agate and keep it with you throughout the course of one day (in your bag or beside you on your desk, for example), then at night place it under your bed. In the morning, hold the stone close to your third eye (in between your eyebrows) and say, 'Thank you, Mélusine, for your comfort and your forgiving heart.'

Themed Oracles

ROMANTIC RELATIONSHIPS

Give yourself time to forgive someone. Your negative feelings are slowly diminishing day by day, until there will be just a small window of feeling left and you know you have finally let go. Take it at your own pace. The window is open; begin to close it gently.

LIFE PURPOSE

It's not been easy going in the direction you believe is right for you, when others have their own opinions – and often very viable ones. It is time to go your own way, but give thanks for their advice rather than blame them for trying to persuade you otherwise.

FAMILY, FRIENDS AND HOME LIFE

Treasure the way things are on the home front right now, as a little acceptance of what you have, rather than what you wish for, may actually be the way to achieve your goals.

Devana

Key

Wildness.

Oracle

**Be independent, more carefree and less stifled. Consider
your situation with respect for others, but most of all
respect the wild within yourself.**

Myth

Devana was a goddess of wild nature, forests, hunting and the
moon. Known by a variety of names according to local traditions, she can be likened to the Roman goddess Diana and the
Greek goddess Artemis. Devana was seemingly unrestrained and

feisty and one folk tale recounts how she attempted to overthrow Svarog, god of the sun. When Devana's father Perun, the god of thunder, found out, he chased her and cast thunderbolts to scare away her companion wolves. Devana was a shapeshifter, so she transformed into a bird, but Perun turned into an eagle and was about to devour her, so Devana turned into a fish. Eventually, Perun managed to catch her and she had to give up her mad desire to rule the Earth, sun and sky. As a punishment, she was forced to marry the shapeshifting god of the underworld, Veles. At first, Devana despised him, but he temporarily transformed into a basil flower to cast an aroma of sweetness around her and calmed her wild spirit.

Meaning and Wisdom

Audacious and free-spirited, Devana was like many other hunter goddesses – more concerned with her freedom than commitment to anyone or anything. However, her courageous, unruly attitude wreaked havoc on the gods until she met her match in Veles, who shrewdly understood how to win her over. Devana represents that free spirit in all of us that is often activated by the restless energy of the waning moon in Sagittarius. Devana comes into our world to nudge us a little and encourage us to lean into our reckless side, take a risk and wake up our spirit of adventure. After all, if you don't try, you'll never know.

Her Message

Are you bold and carefree, or restrained? Are you perhaps living only by the rules of civilised behaviour or the expectations, opinions and demands of others? Devana has come into your world to invite you to become a free bird and fly away from the constraints and demands of conventional living for a while. Alternatively, she may have come into your life to say you need some calm and it's time to balance the extremist, restless version of yourself with a little soulful time. The wildness in nature doesn't exclude the beauty of its grace. Empower yourself with both.

To Invoke Devana's Lunar Blessing

Take a handful of Devana's sacred basil flowers and scatter them in a small circle on your table. Place a clear quartz or aventurine stone in the centre and say, 'Devana, thank you for the wildness and calmness in nature and for showing me I have the spirit of adventure deep within.' Leave in place for one lunar cycle to invoke Devana's blessing and draw down her power.

Themed Oracles

ROMANTIC RELATIONSHIPS

There is a wild or romantic spark inside you that needs to be lit. Release the flame of your inner spirit into the outer world and enjoy igniting fires around you.

LIFE PURPOSE

You are now courageous, willing to drive away all that is bad in your life, so you can be autonomous and self-determined. Yet there is still one thing stopping you, a fear of failure. See that in that fear you will find its opposite, a fearless trust in yourself. Act now and be rewarded.

FAMILY, FRIENDS AND HOME LIFE

One family member or friend is perhaps kidding themselves about what they can achieve, or what they think they can't do. Be bold and restore their faith in themselves, by showing them the power of your own motivation.

The Morrígan

Tradition: Irish/Celtic
Symbols: crow, cattle, snake, lunar cycle, triple
goddess
Lunar cycle: waxing moon in Aries
Sacred crystals: bloodstone, red jasper
Keywords: transformation, courage, truth, power,
self-confidence

Key

Authority.

Oracle

**When all seems lost is when selfhood is found through
strength and determination. It is time to rediscover your
inner sovereign.**

Myth

The stories of the Morrígan are many and complex, but she is best
known as a triple goddess and shapeshifter, associated with war
and battle. She transformed into a carrion crow on the battlefield

and devoured the flesh of dead warriors as a symbol of victory. She is often identified as all three aspects of the Irish goddesses Badb, Macha and Nemain.

As Badb, she was a shapeshifting war goddess, who appeared on the battlefield as the crow, causing fear and confusion among warriors, before choosing which side she favoured and then guiding fallen warriors to the afterlife. As Macha, she was the goddess of war and sovereign goddess of the province of Ulster (a sovereign goddess is specific to Celtic mythology and is usually a protective goddess who marries the king of the territory she personifies), while as Nemain she personified the frenzy, fear and terror of war itself.

It was also believed in Celtic tradition that the Morrígan was a portent of doom, often seen by warriors before they went into battle, washing the bloodstained heads and limbs of those fated to die. If you saw your own head, then you were doomed. Yet she is also considered the source of life, with some scholars suggesting she was rooted in an ancient fertility goddess and was the protector of both Ulster and the dead.

Meaning and Wisdom

The Morrígan is a sign to be aware of your own sovereignty – in other words, your power, your dignity, your pride. To care and protect your 'winning side' and to let the death of your old self, or your 'losing side', remain in the past. If this sounds hard, it is because it is meant to be. The Morrígan warns you of what might be if you neglect yourself. Now is the time to be a warrior for your cause, and the Morrígan emphasises the strength and leadership that can be found during the waxing moon in Aries phase. In one myth, the Morrígan promised success in war to the Dagda, a great god in Irish mythology, if he slept with her. He agreed and she frightened away the enemy to bring about his success. In another myth she offered the same favours to the hero Cú Chulainn, who turned her down, and her vengeful actions led to his death. It is for you to decide if you fight with the Morrígan or against her. Let her into your world and she will favour yours.

Her Message

Some people have physical courage, others have emotional courage, and many of us don't tap into either of these innate skills because fear takes over. The Morrígan asks you to see fear itself as your battlefield. What do you fear most? What is the trigger for your fear and what battles do you avoid? The Morrígan tells you that no matter how much it may overwhelm you, fear is an illusion. And yet, ironically, we all 'fear' fear. But it is possible to accept fear without letting it consume you. Face fear head on and choose to work with it; having the courage to do so will allow you to become fearless.

To Invoke the Morrígan's Lunar Blessing

To ensure the Morrígan encourages you to work with your fears or become a warrior for your own power, leave her an offering. Draw a triple moon goddess symbol on a piece of paper and place a red crystal on each of the three phases of the moon. Gaze at your offering, and then say:

> *Welcome the Morrígan, to help me overcome all fear,*
> *And to take back my sovereignty.*
> *With wild crow and raven's dignity,*
> *Return this favour, so blessed be.*

Leave the offering for one lunar cycle to encourage the Morrígan's empowering blessing.

Themed Oracles

ROMANTIC RELATIONSHIPS

Fight for what you believe in. If a lover or partner is not in agreement with you, then now is the time to be true to your own conviction. You need to show you have a right to your beliefs. Courage is all.

LIFE PURPOSE

Do you fear moving on and leaving what you have behind? Or do you want to run away, escape from a difficult lifestyle, but find that something is holding you back? Now is not a time to linger, push forward and start afresh – leave your unwanted baggage behind.

FAMILY, FRIENDS AND HOME LIFE

There may be a struggle for power in your family life. Someone is trying to rule the roost or claims they know what's best for everyone else, but in fact they don't know what's best for themselves. Don't intervene but think things through shrewdly with everyone's best interests in mind.

Circe

Tradition: Ancient Greek
Symbols: wand, chalice, moly root/snowdrop,
  kestrel, wild beasts
Lunar cycle: dark of the moon in Taurus
Sacred crystals: black tourmaline, onyx, emerald
Keywords: solitude, self-possession, power,
  independence

Key

Self-reliance.

Oracle

**Don't try to possess others or rely on them to feel loved.
If you find it within you to love others unconditionally,
you will find boundless love takes the place of feeling
bound by love.**

Myth

The daughter of the sun god Helios and the sea nymph Perse, Circe
is renowned for falling in love with gods and mortals alike. When

betrayed or rejected, she used the art of witchcraft to seek revenge. She transformed the king of Latium, Picus, into a woodpecker for resisting her advances, and when rejected by the sea god Glaucus, who was in love with the nymph Scylla, Circe poisoned Scylla's favourite bathing lagoon, turning her into a terrifying monster.

When Odysseus was shipwrecked on Circe's island of Aeaea, she used her powers to turn half of his men into pigs and other wild animals. Odysseus, however, resisted the same fate with the help of Hermes, who instructed him to take moly root (thought to be snowdrop) to nullify Circe's magic. Circe gradually fell in love with Odysseus and transformed his crew back to their human form, and Odysseus too reciprocated her affection. In various accounts, he spent several happy years with her on the island and fathered three children. But Odysseus felt duty-bound to return home to Ithaca and his wife, Penelope. Circe, although heartbroken that he had to leave, advised him on the safest route to take and how to avoid the sea monster, Scylla. She waved goodbye with great sadness, hoping one day he might return to her island.

Meaning and Wisdom

Some accounts suggest that the name Circe is derived from the Greek word *kirke* meaning 'to secure with rings' and perhaps refers to the binding power of magic (although other sources believe it is a name for a falcon or female kestrel). Circe's nature seems to align with both the binding power of witchcraft and the binding, possessive power of the dark of the moon in Taurus. Although Circe was fiercely independent, she was still capable of empathy and compassion for the suffering of Odysseus's men, and Odysseus's yearning to continue his voyage. So, what does this mean for you? Circe comes to tell you to dedicate yourself to working with your gifts to benefit others, instead of using them in a negative way to bind others to you or prey on them. She represents the quality of self-reliance and tells us not to depend on the love of others to make us feel complete.

Her Message

How often do you feel rejected? Not just in love, but maybe on social media when no one likes your post? You wish you could do something else to warrant notice or receive a signal that someone is thinking of you. We all have a Circe inside us – a desire to lure others to us, perhaps to make us feel good about ourselves or heal a wound or loss, or to compensate for our own vulnerability. Circe welcomes you to her lonely island and invites you to see that personal power isn't just about wielding magic to possess or control others, but about integrity and self-possession. Circe's message reminds you to accept the darker nature within you, the shadow side of you that includes all the parts you often deny, repress or ignore. The shadow that lies within us all. Open up to the dark of the soul, listen to Circe's words, and embrace your authentic self. That way, you can bring the shadows into the light, and you can be true to who you are.

To Invoke Circe's Lunar Blessing

Use these sacred words to call on Circe as you turn your face to the moon:

I won't dance in the darkness of knots and ties,
They'll bind me, they'll wrap me, they'll fill me with lies.
I'll untangle this web, so look in my eyes,
With Circe's power, I'm fearless and wise.

After you have recited your message, encourage Circe's self-sustaining power by drawing a circle on a piece of paper and writing in the centre, 'Thank you Circe for your gifts of resilience and fortitude'. Then draw an image of a snowdrop (to represent moly root) beside your words to seal your intention for her blessing.

Themed Oracles

ROMANTIC RELATIONSHIPS

You may be attracted to something or someone unattainable and feel you can't free yourself from that attraction. Being bound by the chains of love means you are relinquishing your own power. Don't give up on yourself, give all your love to yourself instead.

LIFE PURPOSE

It is likely you have been going down a pathway directed by other people's expectations, but you need to choose your own way forward. You may feel alone in this, but if you are sure of your goal, then nothing will stop you achieving it.

FAMILY, FRIENDS AND HOME LIFE

You need to get to the root of someone's unease or emotional distance. Are they hiding something or fearful of revealing something important because of your reaction? Objectivity is needed now.

Frigg

Tradition: Norse
Symbols: mistletoe, spinning wheel, silver, winter
Lunar cycle: waning moon in Scorpio
Sacred crystals: black tourmaline, onyx
Keywords: secrets, concealment, hidden feelings

Key

Secrecy.

Oracle

A secret must remain a secret. Follow your intuition and don't give anything away, however much you believe you trust in someone. Secrets are best kept that way.

Myth

The queen of Asgard and the wife of the god Odin, Frigg is associated with marriage, prophecy, the moon and motherhood, and lived in Fensalir, the Hall of the Marshlands. Her most devoted attendant, Fulla, wore a gold chaplet in her long fair hair and was the guardian of Frigg's casket of magical slippers and secrets.

Mother to the fair and wise god, Baldr, Frigg was a prophetess and foresaw his early death in a dream. She secretly attempted to change his fate by demanding that all living things were never to harm him – but there was one thing that she didn't include: mistletoe. The trickster Loki despised Baldr and, wanting to see him doomed, dressed up as a woman so he could get close to Frigg at her court. Loki, in disguise, brought Frigg news of Baldr, telling her that he was invulnerable to whatever was thrown or shot at him and asking how Frigg managed to work such magic. Frigg told Loki that she had asked every living thing never to harm him, except mistletoe, because it seemed too fragile to do her son any damage. So, Loki made an arrow out of mistletoe and gave it to Baldr's blind brother, Hodhr. When out hunting with Baldr, Hodhr was directed by Loki to shoot the arrow straight at his brother, killing him. Frigg was distraught and her tears turned to white berries, which according to legend, covered the mistletoe plant as a symbol of her love for him.

Meaning and Wisdom

Frigg was a woman of secrets. She had a box full of slippers that were said to be magical, and she could see the future, but she never spoke of it. She was said to have had affairs with some of her siblings, yet none were mentioned publicly, and we know that she secretly tried to save her son. But her devotion to Baldr's safety was in vain, because there was a trickster in her midst who saw through her ruse and uncovered her secret. Likewise, you should never reveal a secret during the waning moon in Scorpio or it will be used against you. Frigg tells us to keep our secrets hidden, for a secret is only a secret when it is not shared. Frigg reminds us to devote our time to being honest and open when we need to, but to cherish and honour our secret world too.

Her Message

Do you have secrets? Perhaps experiences from the past that you would never dare divulge to others? Perhaps secret desires, actions or intentions that are considered taboo or just unattainable? And if so, do you keep these secrets safe? Are they locked in a symbolic mental casket, tucked away at the back of your mind? Or do these secrets sometimes slip out and seem to arrive magically on the tip of your tongue? Frigg comes into your life to remind you that – especially during a waning moon, when we let down our guard a little – it can be easy to let your tongue slip, to drop a hint or even signal unconsciously to someone that you have a secret, which can be a powerful draw for others to attempt to trick you into revealing all. Frigg reminds you to be careful when people say, 'Your secret's safe with me.' Because it never is.

To Invoke Frigg's Lunar Blessing

To protect your secrets and invoke Frigg's blessing, create your own protective casket. Stand facing the direction of the moon and trace with your finger an imaginary circle of protection around you in an anti-clockwise direction. Close your eyes and imagine this circle of safety, always around you, wherever you go. Whoever you are with will not be able to cross into your space; this is your secret space and no one knows about it. Tell no one of this secret space and your secrets will be safe.

Themed Oracle

ROMANTIC RELATIONSHIPS

A recent conversation brought to light something significant. It would be enlightening to recall what that was; it will help you to realise what you truly want and where you are going in a relationship.

LIFE PURPOSE

There are many secret desires in your heart, but you've been struggling to decide which is the right one to follow. See beyond the obvious route; look from different perspectives and a hidden desire will come to light.

FAMILY, FRIENDS AND HOME LIFE

An aura of mystery surrounds you and it's hard for family or friends to see clearly what you truly need. Make it clear how much you value their advice, but you must go it alone when making decisions for your future.

Yèmọja

Tradition: Yoruba
Symbols: Fish, mermaid, blue, rivers, shells
Lunar cycle: full moon in Gemini
Sacred crystals: pearl, shells, aquamarine
Keywords: protean, adaptable, changeable,
  whimsical

Key

Versatility.

Oracle

Embrace the changes that are to come. Hug them close to you as if they were your long-lost friends and join in the joy of their camaraderie.

Myth

Note: Yèmọja's name and worship vary according to geographical location and tradition. For example, she is known as Iamanja in Brazil and as Yemonja in the Òrìọàs religion of the Caribbean.

Yèmọja, meaning 'fish mother', was originally a water goddess of the Yoruba tradition, originating in present-day Nigeria. In addition to mothering fourteen (or some say eleven) òrìọàs or spirits, as well as the sun and moon, she also gave birth to all of Earth's bodies of water. The mother goddess and protector of the West African Ogun River, she is also the ocean goddess in Cuban and Brazilian òrìọàs traditions, and as moon goddess, she rules tides, fertility and women's cycles. Like many other ocean and water deities, she is an ambivalent spirit. When angered she can be destructive, creating floods, tsunamis or turbulent rivers, yet she is also comforting and kind with her gentle surf, her bountiful fishing resources and her life-giving waters in springs and freshwater streams. As the protector of women, she is worshipped for healthy children, love, healing and good luck. She is usually depicted as a mermaid and associated with the colour blue.

Meaning and Wisdom

Yèmọja is a goddess of many faces. Not only has she a range of aspects according to local traditions, in herself she is protean, changeable and as unpredictable as the sea, just like the full moon in Gemini. Yèmọja encourages you to swim with the tide, rather than against it. To go with the flow, let change and unpredictability be as nurturing as the tried and trusted, and to be as diverse as the goddess herself, who is found across the oceans worldwide in different guises. She is all-encompassing and all-giving, but in her essence she is a water goddess who is as changeable as the moon.

Her Message

Yèmọja reminds us that life isn't just up and down, yes and no, yin and yang. In fact, there are grey areas, ifs and buts and endless possibilities to consider. The only constant in life is change. If you are ready to go with the flow of this change, to see the undercurrents as well as what lies on the surface, you may uncover hidden depths within you that will allow you to experience the joy you seek.

To Invoke Yèmọja's Lunar Blessing

During a full moon phase, offer Yèmọja petitions of fruit, wine, bread or water. Yèmọja listens to all of us; she doesn't take sides or judge and she welcomes each and every one of us so that we can discover comfort, joy and our own pathway to good luck. Show you embrace her oceanic and lunar power through your own offerings and say, 'Thank you, Yèmọja, for your gift of versatility.'

Themed Oracles

ROMANTIC RELATIONSHIPS

You need to focus and find clarity about what a relationship means to you. Even if you are restricted by current circumstances or your own lack of direction or courage, you do have choices and there is a way out. Don't let a tidal wave of feeling overwhelm you, overcome it instead.

LIFE PURPOSE

There are simply too many choices and Yèmoja tells you to be objective and follow your intuition. Any way forward is a step in the right direction. Make a decision and stick to it, rather than prevaricating or trying to find a way out of making a choice.

FAMILY, FRIENDS AND HOME LIFE

There is nothing wrong with saying, 'I don't know.' Don't give in to pressure, take your time to let the answer come to you.

Diana

Tradition: Roman
Symbols: crescent waxing moon, stag, shield,
   chariot, bow and quiver, willow
Lunar cycle: waxing moon in Gemini
Sacred crystals: moonstone, citrine
Keywords: adaptability, crossroads, juggling,
   choice

Key

Flexibility.

Oracle

Bend, don't break. This is the time to remain self-possessed and flow with the moon's ever-changing energy. Be flexible and adapt to the circumstances of the moment.

Myth

Diana was an indigenous ancient Italian goddess of the woodlands. Her worship as Diana of Nemi was established near Lake Nemi in the Alban Hills, not far from Rome, around 600 BCE, and a temple was dedicated to her there around 300 BCE. As her cult spread, she acquired attributes of other goddesses, such as the Greek Artemis and Hecate, and the Roman moon goddess, Luna. A virgin goddess of childbirth and fertility, Diana remained aloof and enjoyed the solitude of the wild groves and springs of the forest. Men were forbidden to enter her temple on the Aventine Hill in Rome. Diana is a multifaceted goddess who adapted to the times and the different cults with which she became associated. She probably originated from an ancient Earth goddess (as with her Greek equivalent, Artemis) and was assimilated into the Roman pantheon as the daughter of Jupiter and Latona (or the Greek Zeus and Leto) along with her brother, Apollo, god of light.

Meaning and Wisdom

Diana was a wild huntress and a protectress of wildlife, women in childbirth and slaves. She was also worshipped as a goddess of fertility. In a way, she remains an enigma – there are few stories surrounding her, such is her elusive nature, yet she is respected and honoured for her hunting prowess. She was given the epithet of Trivia (meaning 'three ways' and referring to a three-way cross-road or junction), and in this aspect she asks us to adapt and take another direction that may unexpectedly call out to us, even if it's not the one we first thought was right.

When Diana appears in your life, she is here to tell you to stay poised and guard your composure, to adapt to circumstances, but to see the way forward for yourself.

Her Message

When we arrive at a crossroads, we need to choose which way to go. Often, we have a map, ready to follow the direction we were intent on taking or the easiest route. But sometimes we have to make choices in the dark, without the help of a guiding map. So, Diana comes to you to remind you to bend with the wind, to flow with the current, to be flexible and open to change, to remain a little wild and never be tamed, and to embrace your inner bliss. When the moon is waxing in adaptable Gemini, it gives us the chance to see other pathways we may not have noticed before. Similarly, Diana illuminates possibilities, changes and the unpredictable, not the road itself. The more you are ready and open to the unknown, the more likely you are to discover your true pathway.

To Invoke Diana's Lunar Blessing

You can do this at any time of day when you feel safe to stand at the crossing of three pathways.

As you stand, realise you have the power to choose which road to go down. No matter where it leads, it will be the right choice.

Place a small branch, twig or stem of a plant at the junction as a petition for Diana's blessing, then walk down the path you have chosen for as long as you feel is right, intuitively. Be aware of how good you feel as you make that choice. Next time you have a decision to make, imagine this moment and realise that whatever choice you do make is the right one for that moment, for you were in a place of *ataraxia* or complete serenity.

Themed Oracles

ROMANTIC RELATIONSHIPS

Look for new ways to handle a co-dependent relationship that's keeping you from moving forward. Adapt, juggle the options, but stick to what is true for you and that way you can navigate your pathway through the tangled forest that love is.

LIFE PURPOSE

There are so many possibilities in life, don't waste your time wondering which way to turn. Just go in the direction that feels right for you now. There is always another crossroads ahead and another choice to make.

FAMILY, FRIENDS AND HOME LIFE

You may be juggling several family or social issues at once, so now is the time to see how you can navigate disparate demands or deal with changing scenarios, especially if you stay flexible and open to change.

Hanwi

Key

Dignity.

Oracle

**As if taking a fine thread of gold to work into a tapestry,
imagine a golden light shining into you and the light of
self-worth shining out.**

Myth

Meaning 'night sun', Hanwi is the moon spirit or goddess in
Indigenous American mythology, guarding her people during the
night and protecting them from evil spirits.

The sun god Wi, married to Hanwi, was mesmerised by the beauty of the mortal Ite, the wife of the wind god, and asked Ite to take Hanwi's place beside him at a banquet of the gods. When Hanwi arrived, everyone laughed at her because she had been replaced by a mere mortal, so she turned her face away in humiliation. The sky god Skan, who judged all the other gods for their treatment of Hanwi, punished Wi by allowing Wi to rule the day, while Hanwi could rule the night. She is often seen hiding part of her face from the shame of his betrayal (the half-moon), yet at times her face is fully revealed (the full moon) in the light of pure self-respect and dignity.

Meaning and Wisdom

Hanwi's myth reflects our sense of humiliation when we are called out or made a fool of. But she also reminds us that this is really a test of our ability to remain strong in the face of a breach of trust. If we are open to Hanwi's oracle, her light and wisdom penetrate our negativity, protecting us from dark feelings. She also tells us that even if we have been disrespected, it is through giving value to our sense of dignity that the revived light of self-esteem shines again. When the full moon is in Pisces, all our vulnerabilities, sensitivities and feelings are heightened, so Hanwi comes to help us clear our minds of negativity and reassures us that we are safe while she watches over us.

Her Message

Hanwi comes to remind you about your vulnerable side and how sometimes we all feel ashamed of having feelings or emotional reactions that spring from that vulnerability. Is someone calling you out when you wanted to keep everything in the dark? Hanwi tells you that it's time to honour and accept feelings for what they are. It's how you react to those feelings that will determine your future. If, however, like Hanwi, someone else humiliated you through no fault of your own, then now is the time to free yourself from self-reproach and replace it with a sense of self-belief.

To Invoke Hanwi's Lunar Blessing

Make a circle of stones somewhere outdoors to represent the full moon, to draw down the power of Hanwi. Stand in front of your circle and say, 'Bless you, Hanwi, for your protection and for lighting the pathway to finding my self-esteem.' Then, throw one more stone into the circle. This represents you and how you are now aligned with the lunar cycle, ready for Hanwi's encouragement and influence.

Themed Oracles

ROMANTIC RELATIONSHIPS

Be selfless, but don't be selfish; be wonderful, but be in wonder; be open, but maintain your boundaries. In fact, now is the time to be in awe of the power you possess and the power of love, as a relationship is being charged with Hanwi's full-moon light.

LIFE PURPOSE

You have the intention to go down a particular route, yet it seems that others are giving you a hard time about your decision. It might be easier to turn your face away, shrug your shoulders and give up on your plan. But only you know what's best for you, so don't give up on knowing what you truly desire.

FAMILY, FRIENDS AND HOME LIFE

Hold out a hand to welcome others into your world. They need your respect and acceptance right now, so be prepared to cast a moonlit ray of trust into the mix and mutual respect will be your reward.

Dido

Tradition: Ancient Greek/Roman
Symbols: fire, sword, crown, lion
Lunar cycle: waning moon in Leo
Sacred crystals: tiger's eye, sunstone, red carnelian
Keywords: redemption, responsibility, choice

Key

Redemption.

Oracle

Take responsibility for your actions. Whatever your pain or regret, you can choose to forgive, forget and move on. Banish all resentment; redemption is your gift.

Myth

Also known as Elissa, Dido was the legendary queen of Carthage (c.814 BCE). According to most accounts, Dido escaped from her ruthless brother Pygmalion after she discovered he had assassinated her husband, Sychaeus, in order to seize his wealth. Fleeing to Africa, she founded Carthage and the city prospered. She is often recognised as a figure in Virgil's epic poem, the *Aeneid* (20 BCE), which tells the story of the Trojan hero, Aeneas. According to Virgil, Aeneas arrived in Carthage after seven years wandering the seas with his fleet. While listening to Aeneas recount his experiences of the Trojan War, Dido fell madly in love and at first it seemed her feelings were reciprocated.

But Dido had vowed never to love again following the death of her husband. Torn between her duty to the people of Carthage and her passion for Aeneas, she suggested that the Trojans settle in Carthage and that she and Aeneas reign jointly over their people. Aeneas and his men stayed for nearly a year, before the gods sent the messenger Mercury to remind Aeneas that he had to continue his journey, for that was his fate. Dido discovered he was leaving and, rejected, humiliated and guilt-ridden for the betrayal of her husband, she prayed at her shrine for her own death, then put a curse on Aeneas that would ultimately culminate in the Punic Wars. On her ready-prepared funeral pyre, Dido then stabbed herself with Aeneas's Trojan sword.

Meaning and Wisdom

This tragic tale of human love, duty, guilt and broken promises poses many questions about betrayal, love and fate. Aeneas left Dido without telling her, guilt-ridden but believing he must follow the call of the gods, his fate. But he took a conscious choice to resign himself to accept his fate. Similarly, we may believe we are fated to do this or that, or even feel 'fatally' attracted to someone, but we have the power to change our so-called fate through our choices. The only way Dido believed she could redeem herself for betraying her husband was by ending her own life. Dido would not forgive herself, nor would she forgive Aeneas, but she did have the free will to make those choices.

Her Message

Later in the *Aeneid*, Aeneas has to descend into the underworld to search for his father Anchises, and there he encounters Dido as 'a ghost who died of love'. He begs her to stay with him, telling her he left her unwillingly, but she runs towards her ghost husband instead, who 'meets her love with love'. Perhaps this encapsulates the most important message that Dido comes to tell you, that true love is eternal, it is an energy, a force of its own that transcends human existence. It permeates our lives through passion, sexual desire, physical longing, comfort, gentleness and care, but it also comes wrapped in memories of what love once meant to us and how it can return to us again. As the moon wanes in loving Leo, love can desert you, but as the moon waxes again, so too can love grow and flourish. Love is like the moon and Dido reminds you to learn to go with love's flow, in and out of your life. To forgive and to give again.

To Invoke Dido's Lunar Blessing

Light a red tea-light candle as an offering to Dido and thank her by saying, 'Bless you for showing me the way to cherish personal autonomy.' Blow out the candle when you are ready and reflect on the value in self-forgiveness – the one thing Dido could not do.

Themed Oracles

ROMANTIC RELATIONSHIPS

Now you have a choice to make in a love relationship. It is with free will that you make this choice – because no matter how much you might believe you have no choice, there is always a path open to you.

LIFE PURPOSE

You may feel that external influences are stopping you from achieving your goals. But the roadblocks are there to slow you down a little, to encourage you to stop and reflect before you act too soon. Take your time to choose your path freely and willingly.

FAMILY, FRIENDS AND HOME LIFE

Strength and determination are needed now to make it clear what behaviour is acceptable and what is not. Don't let someone manipulate you, nor let them carry on doing something reprehensible without a justifiable reason for their actions.

Luna

Tradition: Roman
Symbols: chariot, water, torch, oxen, fertility,
  childbirth
Lunar cycle: full moon in Sagittarius
Sacred crystals: moonstone, lapis lazuli,
  aquamarine
Keywords: completion, full circle, change, wheel of
  fortune

Key

Fulfilment.

Oracle

**Each day I, Luna, grow in strength, until I am ripe and
ready to give all that I have. I come to give you the power
of change, renewal and completion. Use it wisely.**

Myth

Associated with the ancient Italian goddess Anna Perenna and the
Greek goddess Selene, Luna occupied a key position in Roman

religion as the source of their lunar calendar calculations. Luna had her own temples on the Aventine and Palatine Hills and at the latter she was called Noctiluca ('night-shiner'), her temple lit up with torches every night in her honour. Anna Perenna was the moon goddess of the complete lunar cycle, while Luna represented the full moon as part of the moon goddess triad of Diana (waxing moon) and Hecate (waning/dark of the moon). She was also associated with other goddesses linked to chastity and childbirth such as Proserpina and Juno Lucina, an ancient mother goddess who protected the lives of women in labour. Ruling the moon, agriculture, femininity, childbirth, the wind, rain, tides, wildlife and the seas, when worshipped, Luna brings us fulfilment, good fortune and a sense of completion.

Meaning and Wisdom

Luna seems to embody many different faces of the moon and her goddesses. Yet who was she really and what does she mean to us? She may have been a Roman version of the Greek Selene, or conflated with Anna Perenna and Diana, but her name is a testament to her power. Her wisdom is in her ever-changing but repeating cycle, reminding us of our own life cycle and other natural, planetary, cosmic or seasonal cycles. Like the self-driven but changeable influence of the full moon in Sagittarius, Luna comes into your life to tell you to accept the only constant in life is change and to find fulfilment in every moment, as every moment moves us on to the next one.

Her Message

Luna's epithet as 'night-shiner' acts as a reminder to shine a light, metaphorically, on the parts of you that are in shadow. Ask yourself, what does being fulfilled mean to you? What, right now, would encourage a sense of fulfilment, and how are you going about evoking it? Rather than resisting, go with the flow of any external changes and embrace the idea that change itself is a fulfilling experience. This night-shiner brings you the gift of seeing what you truly need to change in your life for a sense of happiness.

To Invoke Luna's Lunar Blessing

Make a votive offering to Luna to welcome her blessing by piling up a small mound of stones to represent the full moon's culminating energy. As you place the last stone on top, thank the goddess for bringing you her lunar wisdom by saying, 'Luna's light has come to me so that I can embrace change, so let it be.'

Themed Oracles

ROMANTIC RELATIONSHIPS

This is a time when one love connection is under the spotlight, as the moon shines brightly upon the truth. In the light, welcome the shadows; in the darkness, welcome the light of clarity.

LIFE PURPOSE

Stop hesitating, jump on the wheel of fortune and let it whirl you around like you're on a roundabout. Be ready to jump off when you see the pathway meant for you. If you don't know what that is now, you will discover it very soon.

FAMILY, FRIENDS AND HOME LIFE

You want something different to happen. You have itchy feet. You're restless and edgy, but the time has come to step forward across that line of hesitation and act on instinct.

Nyx

Tradition: Ancient Greek
Symbols: stars, wings, chariot, mists, night
Lunar cycle: dark of the moon in Cancer
Sacred crystals: sapphire, onyx, black tourmaline
Keywords: obscurity, concealment, mystery

Key

Mystery.

Oracle

Something about you seems to be hidden, unknown. Now is the time to embrace your enigmatic self and discover your own mystery.

Myth

Nyx was said to be one of the primordial deities at the dawn of creation, emerging from Chaos. Coupling with her brother Erebus (darkness), she produced Aether (light) and Hemera (day). She also mothered the Fates, these being Clotho, Lachesis and Atropos, and also Hypnos, Eris and Nemesis. Orphic cosmology, the cult of Orpheus, described her as the source of all life, bringing calm and peace to the world. While the darkness of Nyx could be fearful, she was also welcomed for her stillness and ability to send prophetic, beautiful dreams.

Meaning and Wisdom

Nyx aligns to the dark of the moon in Cancer, a time when we may feel immersed in our emotions and feelings, but it is also a time when we can reach inwards and begin to understand the unfathomable depths of our own mystery. This is when Nyx rejoices and sends us her gift of concealment, when her dark cloak covers the moon's loveliness, and the moon – untouched by the light of the sun – reveals only mystery.

Nyx comes with twinkling stars shining around and through her, reminding you to treasure the stars that lie within you too. This is the ineffable, incredible and undefinable place of our deepest selves, and Nyx beseeches you to embrace that mystery. Is there a mystery in your life that you are trying to unravel? Or are you constantly trying too hard to be in the know about everything? If so, Nyx comes to remind you that there is more in life than cause and effect; there is more than analysis and facts. In fact, there is all that is 'unknown' too. Now is the time to open yourself to the unknown and to realise that if you gaze up into the canopy of the night, you will find your own mystery written there in the stars.

Her Message

Nyx reminds you that caring about the mysteries of life and the universe will nurture your soul and are just as important as the day-to-day truths. Nyx's daughter, Hemera, represents the logical world of facts and figures, but we can't always find the answers we are searching for or manifest our desires with logic alone. Even in the light of day, we still have to honour our deeper feelings and trust in visceral instinct. So, let Nyx bring you her gift of darkness and – even if you are the most open and honest individual on the planet – don't always feel you have to tell all. Immerse yourself in a little mystery of your own. You don't have to demystify or clarify every situation. Nyx asks you to embrace mystery for what it is: the unknown.

To Invoke Nyx's Lunar Blessing

Light a white tea-light candle and a black tea-light candle to represent day and night. Focus first on the white candle and say, 'For now, Hemera, spirit of the daylight, be gone until the morning comes.' Then blow out the candle. Turn to the black candle and say, 'For now, Nyx, goddess of the dark, I welcome you until daylight comes again.' Then blow out the black candle to show you have aligned to the balance of night and day. Finish the ritual by saying:

Nyx, here in your darkness I see the truth of who I am and welcome your guidance, wisdom and sacred presence, always above me, your cloak of night protecting me in the dark. Thank you for your mysterious power

Themed Oracles

ROMANTIC RELATIONSHIPS

A secret will soon be revealed, but don't try and uncover the truth yourself. For just as daylight comes when the sun rises, so too will illumination displace mystery.

LIFE PURPOSE

You've been in the dark about what you truly want and where you're going. Although you may have seen glimpses through the mists of confusion and other people's expectations, the path forward has been hazy at best. But soon the mist will dissipate and all will become clear.

FAMILY, FRIENDS AND HOME LIFE

Sometimes in the darkest places we find the light and all home and family matters that have been confusing or hidden will now become clear, as the stars of revelation shine through the dark night of confusion.

Selene

Key

Passion.

Oracle

To live with passion in your heart and soul is to be alive.

Myth

The Greek moon goddess Selene (also known as Mene) was the sister of Eos, the dawn, and Helios, the sun. Often depicted as driving a chariot across the heavens, led by two or more dazzling white horses or bulls, she was said to have beautiful tresses and was sometimes depicted with a crescent moon diadem.

Selene is best known for her passionate love for the beautiful hunter and shepherd, Endymion. When Selene saw Endymion asleep in a cave, she instantly fell in love with him. Some accounts say that she asked Zeus to put him into an eternal sleep so he would stay young forever and she could visit him every night to make love. According to one source, she became the mother of fifty daughters by him. However, Endymion wasn't the only lover in Selene's world – she had an affair with Zeus (who fathered three of her children, Pandeia, Ersa and Nemea) and the god of the wild, Pan, was also among her lovers.

Meaning and Wisdom

When we think about the moon, it's rare to equate her with intense passion. Often, she's associated with romance, with flowing, fluxing energy, numinous, mystical light, eclipses and magic. Yet the full moon has long been a symbol of madness, of frenzied bacchanalian rites, or simply the madness of our passions. The full moon in Scorpio casts over us a glow of sexual excitement, passion and intensity. Selene cast a spell around Endymion, she became obsessed with him and then became lost in him. Passion is ambiguous; it can be a magical elixir of desire and receptivity, or a confusing one of extreme feeling where we are chained to our desire. Selene reminds us to be passionate, to love intensely, but not to stake our life on someone else.

Her Message

Passion isn't exclusive to love relationships; you could have a lust for work, zeal for a creative skill or just passion for living life to the full. But whatever your passion is, Selene tells you that this feeling, this sense that is so empowering and makes us feel truly alive, can also be dangerous. It can be so captivating that we forget others in our lives and it can be so fierce and all-consuming that we cannot see the reality of that relationship – and anyway, do we even want to? Passion can lead to obsession, and obsession to possession, not only in the sense that we grow possessive of another, but we are possessed by the intensity of the passion itself. In fact, Selene tells us not to sleep through this fervour like Endymion, but awaken to the driving force behind this passion, to what compels you. This will allow you to move forward with clarity and, rather than being blinded by your passion, see it clearly, be at one with it.

If you feel that you have no true passion, then maybe Selene has come to awaken passion within you? This deepest of emotions can heal, can wound, can cure, but can also be a curse. Selene asks you to reflect on what passion means to you and how to direct it to positive results. Yes, live with passion in your soul, let it breathe into you, but don't suffocate on passion. Let it breathe out of you too.

To Invoke Selene's Lunar Blessing

To empower yourself with Selene's positive passion, take some seasonal white flowers and place them in a circle around a moonstone or piece of selenite. Touch the stone with your finger and as you open yourself intuitively to her power, say words such as this traditional invocation: 'Selene, your passion comes to me, to give out my passion and to fill myself with it too. Then passion lives within and without me, but does not possess me.'

Themed Oracles

ROMANTIC RELATIONSHIPS

If you are not already inflamed with passion for someone, then relationship happiness is coming your way. Selene asks you to say this on a moonlit night, to invite and welcome love into your life, and if you already have a passion for someone, repeat the same charm to ensure that passion is your ally, not a foe:

> *Let flames of passion light my way*
> *To greater things each lunar day;*
> *Let love unfurl, not bind us tight,*
> *And set us free with love's true sight.*

LIFE PURPOSE

There is something calling you on, something powerful, necessary and essential to your future happiness. Don't give up on that vision or passion.

FAMILY, FRIENDS AND HOME LIFE

Passion for your home life is brewing. In fact, in the months to come, one particular family dream will be realised, especially if you share your fervour and joy with those around you.

Ix Chel

Tradition: Mayan
Symbols: rainbow, mist, silver, blue
Lunar cycle: waning moon in Aries
Sacred crystals: turquoise, jade
Keywords: fairness, nurturing, preparation, patience

Key

Preparation.

Oracle

Be patient. You are like a gardener preparing the ground, ready for the rains to come and water your seeds of creativity.

Myth

The Mayan goddess of childbirth, healing, the moon, rain, midwifery and fertility, Ix Chel was primarily worshipped at her sanctuary on the island of Cozumel, off the east coast of Yucatán Peninsula. At this sacred site, it was believed a priest would hide inside a large statue of the goddess and offer oracles, mostly to

Mayan women who came to worship the goddess to ensure a fruitful marriage. The goddess was often depicted with an inverted water jar and an entwined serpent headdress. She was thought to invoke both the mystical and wild energy of the jaguar and the lunar aspects of the divine feminine. As a rain deity, she was shown with the waters of creativity flowing from her skirt, while in some accounts the inverted jar was thought to indicate a great flood marking the end of the world. It is now believed among scholars to symbolise her power to create rainstorms and flooding.

Meaning and Wisdom

Ix Chel was associated not only with wild animals, fertility and the moon, but also with oracles. So, what wisdom can she offer? She embodies the message that if you let the metaphorical rain fall upon you, rather than try to take cover from it, you will be blessed with its nourishment. Like the waning moon in Aries, we sometimes have to relinquish our power and let things be. If you are seeking more creativity in your life, then Ix Chel is here to help you give birth to a new idea or plant fresh seeds of success ready for when the rain comes again. In other words, be prepared, watch the weather and trust in the flowing waters from her upturned jar that will forever nourish your garden.

Her Message

Ix Chel says, be patient. The moment of fertilisation, creation or new life is coming very soon. And if you feel any sense of injustice, or that things aren't happening at the speed you would like, then Ix Chel reminds you to welcome her cleansing and nourishing rains. For now, move to the rhythm of your own rain dance to summon Ix Chel's powers and you'll see the fruits of your labour very soon.

To Invoke Ix Chel's Lunar Blessing

Hold a piece of turquoise up to the sky (all the better if it's raining) and say, 'Ix Chel, send me your rains of creative power, your nourishing waters and your jar of plenty. I wait with warmth and goodness for your blessing.'

Themed Oracles

ROMANTIC RELATIONSHIPS

So that you can rebuild a love connection, or instigate a new one, reframe negative thoughts into positive ones and drop any notion that life isn't fair. Fairness is a quality we project onto life, not life onto us. You have the power to make your life as fair as you want it to be.

LIFE PURPOSE

You have a deep need to change your way of thinking, loving or being, but are afraid to admit this to anyone, even yourself.

Whatever you do, don't hang on to the past – this is a possible new beginning. Any change in the wind will bring a gale of vitality into your life and bring you a sense of becoming true to yourself.

FAMILY, FRIENDS AND HOME LIFE

Promise yourself time to be yourself. Don't let family expectations or demands from friends hold you back or prevent you from much-needed 'me time'. Prepare for a lot more self-care and less careless living.

The Sibyl

Tradition: Ancient Greek
Symbols: oak leaf, serpent, smoke, fire,
  sandalwood, mirror
Lunar cycle: waxing moon in Leo
Sacred crystals: red carnelian, citrine, clear quartz
Keywords: forward-thinking, visionary, insightful

Key

Foretelling.

Oracle

Think ahead to what you want to achieve in the future. However unattainable it may seem, the goal will come into focus if you trust in your vision. The more you believe it will happen, the more likely it will manifest.

Myth

Residing in many ancient sacred temples and sites worldwide, oracular priestesses channelled messages from the gods and goddesses and were consulted for their power to foretell the future. In ancient Greece, these priestesses were known as sibyls.

One of the most celebrated sibyls was the Cumaean Sibyl, renowned for selling a collection of oracle texts (known as the Sibylline Books) to the last king of Rome, Lucius Tarquinius Superbus. Tarquinius refused to pay the full amount that the Cumaean Sibyl asked for the nine books, so she retaliated by burning three of them. She again asked for the same amount and the king refused, so she burnt three more of the books. Desperate not to lose them all, Tarquinius ended up paying for nine books even though he was left with only three. The books later became the prized possession of the Roman senate and were regularly consulted for their extraordinary prophecies.

The oracular priestess at Delphi (a temple dedicated to Apollo from the eighth century BCE, but believed to have been built on a site originally dedicated to Gaia) was known as the Pythia. According to the geographer Pausanias, a previous sibyl had resided at Delphi in the eleventh century BCE, but when Apollo took over the temple she was forced to flee and travelled from sacred site to sacred site for hundreds of years. After the wandering sibyl's death, her voice alone continued to travel the lands, singing her oracular riddles wherever she went.

Other sibyls include the Erythraean Sibyl, famous for her prophecy of the coming of Jesus, who gave her oracles in the form of an acrostic.

The Phrygian Sibyl was popularly identified with Cassandra, the Trojan princess who was cursed by Apollo to utter true prophesies that no one would believe. One story recounts how, as a child, Cassandra and her brother Helenus slept in Apollo's temple one night and serpents (probably sent by Apollo) whispered in the children's ears while they were asleep, giving them both the gift of prophecy. The more popular story tells of Apollo falling in love with the beautiful Cassandra and promising that he would grant her the gift of prophecy if she would sleep with him. However, after receiving the gift, Cassandra went back on her word and refused Apollo's advances. The enraged Apollo cursed her so that no one would ever believe a word that she said.

Meaning and Wisdom

The sibyl represents not only an oracle but may manifest as a voice that comes from deep within you to advise you. The waxing moon in Leo is a time when we can rediscover our own creative and divine insight and similarly, the sibyl represents this energy as she comes to urge you to be aware of any flashes of intuition. She also reminds you to look out for signs from the universe. Don't be sceptical like the Trojans, who did not heed Cassandra's warning that the Greeks were hiding in the Trojan Horse and ultimately lost the war. Whether the truth is found in the messages in this book or from deep within, trust your intuition and the symbolic world around you. If you open up to the divine that flows through all things, you can put mystical insight into practice to help you live a more fulfilling life.

Her Message

The sibyl says 'every oracle is a mirror of you' and so guides you to understand yourself better. She also comes to pose a question:

what signs and clues, messages or symbols, in your everyday life, reveal something about you? For example, it could be a moment of synchronicity when you call a friend at exactly the same moment they call you. It could manifest as a moment of insight when you have a vision of yourself doing something amazing in the future. Or it might happen when you get lost on a road trip then find a quicker route than the one you had intended to take. All of these signs are about becoming aware of your intuitive power and they encourage you to find meaning in the symbolic world rather than depending solely on factual information. So, the sibyl tells you to develop and work with the realms of intuition, divination and symbolism to give you meaning in life.

To Invoke the Sybil's Lunar Blessing

To invoke the sybil's blessing, relax and find stillness, then hold your hands in prayer pose at your forehead. Affirm the following: 'I have gifts and qualities that through the light of the moon's radiance, will come to be.' Raise your hands high above your head, still in prayer pose, and look up now to your hands. What one word comes into your mind as you do so? This word is the message of the sibyl's lunar blessing. Carry this word with you in your mind wherever you go and you will soon discover a new direction.

Themed Oracles

ROMANTIC RELATIONSHIPS

There is someone who intuitively knows how you feel, even if you've been keeping it a secret. Whether you believe it or not, soon they will be a huge influence in your life. Equally, you will have an influence over their future too.

LIFE PURPOSE

If you have been thinking about making changes in your life, now is the time to put the ideas into practice. Sometimes we find our way through signs from the universe and now is the time to watch out for such a sign. Whether it's a bird singing a song to you or a chance encounter, let it come into your life to help direct you towards your goal.

FAMILY, FRIENDS AND HOME LIFE

A family member or friend needs some advice, but trust in what your heart is trying to tell you for once, not your head. The only way forward is to be constant in your focus, be sure of your intuition and do not be swayed by others.

Medb

Key

Ambition.

Oracle

**Follow your passion. Heartfelt ambition is the key to
unlocking the door to a chamber of delight.**

Myth

Medb is thought to mean mead-woman or 'she who intoxicates'.
This strong-willed, ambitious, sexually insatiable and legendary
warrior queen of Connacht appears in the Ulster Cycle, a series
of myths in ancient Irish literature. She is the archetypal warrior,
whose cunning, guile and fearlessness were at the core of her

success as a powerful sovereignty goddess. She is thought to have manifested as two queens, Medb of Connacht and Medb of Tara. In ancient Ireland, the drinking of mead – the most popular alcoholic drink of the time – was key to a king's inauguration ceremony. This was when the goddess of the territory would offer him her favours and the mead was used to celebrate their marriage, which bestowed sovereignty upon him.

In one epic tale, known as *Táin Bó Cuailnge* (The Cattle Raid of Cooley), Medb – now married to the King of Connacht, Ailill, after many marriages to previous kings – started a war against the King of Ulster because he wanted to best her husband. Ailill possessed a bull more beautiful and fertile than her own, but Medb heard there was a prize bull in Ulster, owned by a man called Cooley. If she stole the bull, hers would be more valuable than the king's. When Cooley realised that Medb was contemplating taking the bull by force, he was defiant. The unrelenting Medb thought nothing of starting a war to seize the bull to maintain superiority over her husband. The battle ended with Connacht's greatest warrior, Ferdia, being killed, the two bulls goring each other to death and the rest of Medb's army retreating.

As a goddess of extremes, it was believed she had an insatiable sexual appetite, sleeping with as many as thirty men in one day. She also had a sacred tree dedicated to her, and was represented with a squirrel and a raven sitting on her shoulders.

Meaning and Wisdom

When Medb comes into your life, she reminds you, quite forcefully, about what power means to you. Do you equate power with sex, emotion or intellect? Are you driven to be as ambitious and self-promoting as Medb, or are you completely the opposite, feeling unable to elevate yourself, surrounded by people who always seem effortlessly successful? It's timely to see ambition as something to cultivate in your own personal way, and not to compare yourself to others. When the waxing moon transits Taurus, our ambitions can be put to practical use, and Medb reminds you to do just that. Even if your ambition is simply to luxuriate in the world around you, remember Medb languished in her sexual prowess, but was equally delighted by the charm of a squirrel.

Her Message

Whatever your ambition, it is your ambition, no more, no less. So start to come to terms with your true intentions and aspirations. Medb says you don't have to fight others to achieve your goals, but you do need a passion and conviction in what you are doing. You need courage, self-belief, and most of all a strong will to succeed or at least attempt to succeed or achieve whatever it is you have an urge to do, even if you fail. 'If at first you don't succeed, try, try again' may be an old adage, but if you don't even try, you won't ever know the meaning of success.

To invoke Medb's Lunar Blessing

To ensure Medb is on your side, and to bring you courage and the will to succeed in your plans, take a red carnelian or red jasper crystal, wrap it in some apple peel, and bury it in a shallow hole outdoors. Spend the next lunar cycle making plans and starting to put those plans into action. When you feel a sense of achievement, go back and unearth your crystal. If all the peel has decayed, then you are on the road to success; if it still remains, bury the crystal again to invoke Medb's blessing while you continue your quest.

Themed Oracles

ROMANTIC RELATIONSHIPS

A relationship isn't all that you want it to be. Perhaps there is inequality, one more involved than the other, or more intense than was intended. Whatever the case, it is timely to redress the balance by being honest about both your needs.

LIFE PURPOSE

You know where you are going and why. In fact, you're so sure of the outcome that nothing is going to stop you. The only obstacle in your way is not listening to important advice that is about to be given to you.

FAMILY, FRIENDS AND HOME LIFE

Someone supports you no matter what, but it feels like they don't actually understand your concerns. Show your passion and that you are only human, not a legendary queen.

Mohini

Tradition: Hindu
Symbols: lotus flower, trident, ocean, tiger
Lunar cycle: dark of the moon in Gemini
Sacred crystals: citrine, opal, tiger's eye
Keywords: beguilement, illusion, seduction

Key

Enchantment.

Oracle

Dance to the music of time. Welcome enchantment into your life and free yourself from your inner demons.

Myth

The female avatar (manifestation of a deity) of the Hindu god Vishnu, Mohini is the goddess of bewitchment and illusion. She is often depicted as a seductive dancer who entices demons, usually leading them to their doom. In the epic Sanskrit tale the *Mahabharata*, Mohini seduces the greedy *asuras* (demons) and steals a pot of their *amrita* (the elixir of immortality). She gives it to the gods to help them triumph over the demons. In a later text known as *Vishnu Purana*, the demon known as Bhasmasura worships the great god Shiva. In return, Shiva grants him the power to turn anyone to ashes just by touching their head. The sly demon decides to work his newfound power on Shiva himself. Shiva prays to Vishnu for help and Vishnu transforms into Mohini, who seduces Bhasmasura. The demon then asks her to marry him and Mohini agrees, but only on the condition that Bhasmasura does exactly as she says as they dance. In the course of the mesmeric dance, she places her hand on her head and Bhasmasura, enchanted by her beauty, mimics the action and reduces himself to ashes.

Meaning and Wisdom

We all have inner demons that often come to light during the dark of the new moon phase in Gemini. These are the bits of ourselves we don't like very much, including traits that we perceive to be negative, and our thoughts and fears, which we might feel we need to suppress. Mohini casts a spell on these demons, entrancing, seducing and tempting them so that she can nullify their power. Sometimes our inner demons threaten to overwhelm us, so we must also learn to resist their power like Mohini.

Her Message

Mohini comes to tell you to always follow your heart, even if the people around you might disapprove. Be as liberated as the goddess and free yourself from the localised demons of the mind, such as fear, self-doubt or uncertainty, and reduce them to ashes.

To Invoke Mohini's Lunar Blessing

Spontaneously start to dance, now, at this moment, wherever you are. Improvise, rise on your toes, spread your arms, twirl or do the twist, whatever dance you like. As you dance, imagine Mohini is dancing with you. Follow her positions and, if she puts her hand on her head, stop and put your hand on your hip instead – just in case – and listen to her laugh blessing you.

Themed Oracles

ROMANTIC RELATIONSHIPS

Take the lead in the relationship dance and show someone special that you have strength and self-confidence. Your enchanted way of making others feel happy is needed now, and the more you act out the role, the more it will become a natural attribute for mutual success.

LIFE PURPOSE

Look forward to the good times ahead and the more you believe in and visualise your achievement or goal, the more likely it is to manifest. Spread your goodness around and beneficial events and people will come into your world too.

FAMILY, FRIENDS AND HOME LIFE

Sentimental or nostalgic thoughts may cross your mind and it's time to visit people who bring you joy that you may not have seen for some time. They are likely thinking of you too.

Thetis

Culture: Ancient Greece
Symbols: dolphin, seaweed, shells, waves, foam
Lunar cycle: waning moon in Cancer
Sacred crystals: aquamarine, selenite
Keywords: powerlessness, inevitability, fate and
free will

Key

Destiny.

Oracle

We often meet our destiny on the path we take to avoid it.

Myth

Thetis was one of the Nereids, a sea nymph who lived in the deep
ocean and frolicked with dolphins and other sea creatures in her
seaweed robes. Like most sea nymphs she was a shapeshifter,
beautiful and serene. Both Poseidon and Zeus tried to seduce
her, but the goddess Themis prophesied that a son of Thetis
would become more powerful than his father, so both gods had

an immediate change of heart. Instead, Zeus arranged for Thetis to marry a mortal, Peleus, believing that a child fathered by a mortal could never be stronger than any god. Peleus was told he would find Thetis asleep on the beach and if he held her tightly, she wouldn't be able to escape – it was inevitable she would reject him otherwise, according to the gods. Even though Peleus clung tightly to her as she tried to shapeshift and flee, she still managed to transform into a flame, water, a raging lioness and finally a serpent. Peleus managed to hold on to her through all this and she was finally subdued and consented to marry him.

All the gods and goddesses of Olympus were invited to the wedding on Mount Pelion, except for Eris, the goddess of discord, renowned for causing trouble wherever she went. In revenge, Eris stormed into the celebration and threw a golden apple among the guests, inscribed with the words 'to the fairest', knowing this would set off an argument as to who was the most beautiful among the vain goddesses. Zeus intervened and gave the apple to the mortal Paris of Troy to decide. Aphrodite bribed him by offering Paris the most beautiful woman in the world, Helen of Sparta, thus setting in motion the events that led to the Trojan War.

Thetis gave birth to a son, Achilles, but she was consumed by a prophecy that he would die an early but glorious death. In an attempt to protect him, she dipped him in the River Styx to imbue him with immortality. Although most of his body was immersed in the water, Thetis held the baby by the heel, which did not touch the water. This became his vulnerable spot. Still fearful of his fate, she hid Achilles away in the court of King Lycomedes, where Achilles was disguised as a girl in the hope he would be spared from going to war. But when Odysseus arrived at the court in search of him, he easily saw through the disguise and convinced him to join the army of Menelaus, king of Sparta. After Achilles was killed by an arrow that struck his vulnerable heel, Thetis offered his armour to the most courageous Greek left alive at Troy, who – ironically – turned out to be Odysseus. After the loss of her son, Thetis returned to the place she loved best, the sea. Along with the other Nereids, she helped guide the Argonauts safely past the monsters Scylla and Charybdis. When Aesacus, a son of King Priam of Troy, leapt into the sea to drown himself after losing his wife Asterope, Thetis felt pity for the young man and turned him into a seabird.

Meaning and Wisdom

Thetis cared about the painful truth of being a mortal. She cared enough to try and save her son by making him immortal and she cared enough about Aesacus to save him from an untimely death. Everything she did was born out of compassion and a desire to protect, yet she was ultimately unable to change her son's fate. No matter how hard we try, however much we try to escape our fate, it seems we are powerless in the hands of the gods. Yet fate and free will are not mutually exclusive and accepting that they work in tandem can free us from the illusion that either is to blame for our state of being or the choices we make. Similarly, during a waning moon in Cancer phase we may feel that we have no control over the inescapable, but yet this divine force will work with us if we are aware of and respect its presence.

Her Message

Thetis drifts into your life to remind you to think ahead, calmly, and to consider the consequences of your actions. How often do you make snap decisions, make last-minute changes to plans or act without even thinking? We all have moments of impetuosity and we may even later regret our choices. So, Thetis comes to tell you to take a deep breath and reflect, to compose yourself before committing and say, 'I need to think about this.' Having the freedom to reflect means you can make destiny all your own, rather than it owning you.

To Invoke Thetis's Lunar Blessing

Dip your fingers in the surf on a beach (or a bowl of water) and swirl them round and round, plunging your hand a little deeper until the water comes up to your wrist. Then thank Thetis for bringing you composure and serenity as you gently remove your hand and let the drips fall back into the water, imagining her dancing again with the dolphins in the sea.

Themed Oracles

ROMANTIC RELATIONSHIPS

This is a time to reflect carefully on what someone suggests, rather than rashly agreeing. With a little composure and forethought, the outcome will be what you are hoping for.

LIFE PURPOSE

A clear way forward may not be as cut and dried as it appears on paper. Logic isn't always the answer, there is also gut instinct and a deeper knowing that something is of value. Find out what that is before you commit.

FAMILY, FRIENDS AND HOME LIFE

Take a careful look at what needs to be done on a practical level to give you more space from the demands of family or more joy in your social life. It may not be obvious right now, but you soon will begin to transform reassuring ideas into viable projects.

The Cailleach

Tradition: Celtic/Irish/Scottish
Symbols: winter solstice, snow, ice, staff, deer, blue
Lunar cycle: dark of the moon in Capricorn
Sacred crystals: smoky quartz, obsidian, garnet
Keywords: perseverance, determination, wisdom

Key

Overcoming.

Oracle

The winter sun is low and weak, but as it begins to climb higher towards its zenith, remember that you too can raise your spirit and overcome the darkness.

Myth

In Celtic folklore, the Cailleach, also known as the 'veiled one', is the embodiment of both winter and, in some myths, the wild and rugged landscapes of parts of the Gaelic lands. Known in Scottish lore as the Beira, Queen of Winter, this goddess of seasonal wisdom and the cold honest truth is loath to relinquish her icy grip on the land and every year rivals the goddess of spring, Brigid, to ensure winter's continued presence just a little bit longer. Legend tells that if the weather is bad at Imbolc (1 February), then the Cailleach will maintain her wintry hold over the landscape right through to Beltane (1 May). In Gaelic traditions, she is said to have built the mountains for her stepping stones, carried a hammer for shaping the hills and valleys and banged a long stick on the ground to create the valleys. A natural rocky outcrop overlooking the sea in County Cork, known as the Hag of Beara, symbolises the Cailleach's head and shoulders, and it is here that she was thought to have sat in vain waiting for her husband, Manannán mac Lir, the god of the sea, to return to her. She is said to be the mother of all goddesses and gods and can be benevolent to those who respect nature and its changing cycles, but also vengeful or punishing to those who disrupt its balance.

Meaning and Wisdom

The Cailleach, in her aspect of crone (see Triple Goddess, page 81), symbolises winter as we experience it at its gloomiest, during the dark of the moon phase in Capricorn. However, the Cailleach reminds us of the profound connection between nature, wisdom, the cycles of life and how she is most alive when all seems still in the depths of winter. She is tenacious and often merciless as she freezes lakes and water pipes or send gales to rip down roofs and trees.

Yet the Cailleach also protects us by blanketing the land with snow, to let us rest and hibernate in preparation for the busy goings-on of spring and summer. Likewise, the Cailleach reminds us to be strong and determined in all we do – to push on, persevere and never give up our personal crusade, but to accept that as winter gives way to spring, we too must give up the things that will no longer be of any use in our future.

Her Message

When the Cailleach comes into your life, she tells you to take stock of what you have achieved and to respect your future desires, so that you can overcome all of the obstacles you believe may be ahead. As the Cailleach created stepping stones by shaping mountains, you should see any challenges as stepping stones to future happiness, rather than ways to block your route.

The Cailleach is also a symbol of the landscape and the changing power of the seasons, so she comes to remind you of how you too can look to the winter to find wisdom. See how observing and participating in the landscape can change your perception of this time of year, from a period of scarcity to one of beauty and grace. Doesn't that say something about your own 'groundedness', your own connection to the landscape and how you are a part of it too? And if you are a part of the Earth, the landscape and the seasons, you too can bang your staff on the ground to show you can overcome any vulnerabilities and won't be defeated by the winter blues of the past.

To Invoke the Cailleach's Lunar Blessing

Worship the goddess by tapping a piece of wood or a stick three times on the ground and say, 'Welcome, Cailleach. I am ready for your wisdom to empower me.' Then light a blue tea-light candle to welcome her. Watch the flame burn for a few minutes and then, as you blow out the candle, say 'Thank you, Cailleach, for your blessing.'

Themed Oracles

ROMANTIC RELATIONSHIPS

It's hard to change the status quo and move on, but with self-belief and determination for a better romantic life, you will be able to make the changes you truly seek.

LIFE PURPOSE

When the snow gradually thaws and we see the landscape again, we are often surprised at how animated the world is around us, and similarly as problems begin to disappear, your future path will be clearer. There is at last a sense of vibrancy, a feeling that you are mastering your destiny rather than fate controlling you.

FAMILY, FRIENDS AND HOME LIFE

This is not only a time to declutter, change something around or redecorate the home, but to meet new friends, improve your social life or extricate yourself from old friendships that are no longer of any value to your life.

Artemis

Tradition: Ancient Greek
Symbols: deer, bow, arrow, cypress tree, hunting
dog, stag, forest, boar
Lunar cycle: waxing moon in Sagittarius
Sacred crystals: turquoise, clear quartz,
aquamarine
Keywords: freedom-loving, independent,
adventurous

Key

Freedom.

Oracle

**The more you seek freedom, the more you are chained
by the seeking of it. This is the time to let it come to you
without searching for it. Let freedom find you.**

Myth

Known as Mistress of the Animals by the ancient Greeks, Artemis
is one of the most complex and all-encompassing Greek goddesses.

Later identified with Selene, the Greek moon goddess, the Homeric hymn to Artemis sings of her as a 'pure maiden who draws her golden bow' and 'rejoices in the chase, as the tops of the mountains tremble and the tangled wood echoes with the outcry of beasts'. Artemis is essentially a goddess of the wild, of hunting and of the night, and all that seems to ride along with the changing light of the moon. She was petitioned for the protection of women during menstruation and childbirth, both of which are associated with the lunar cycle.

Artemis was a virgin by choice, with some believing she may have preferred women to men. She saved the Cretan goddess of hunting and fishing, Britomartis (see page 117) from a lustful King Minos and was also thought to have loved the Mycenaean princess, Iphigeneia. After killing one of Artemis's sacred stags, the king of Mycenae, Agamemnon, was commanded by Artemis to sacrifice his daughter, Iphigeneia, as recompense. In some accounts of this myth, Artemis instantly fell in love with Iphigeneia just as she was about to be sacrificed and saved her by replacing her with a deer.

But Artemis was vengeful towards anyone who crossed her. For example, Actaeon, the hunter, watched her bathing naked in a pool, so she changed him into a stag who was then torn to pieces by his own hunting dogs. She also caused Narcissus to fall in love with himself and killed Chione, the daughter of Daedalion (a warrior and son of Hesperus, god of the Evening Star), who criticised Artemis's beauty.

Meaning and Wisdom

This paradoxical goddess, who has the capacity for compassion but a will for destruction, is also wild and free, independent and autonomous. Artemis is a hunter, a roamer, adventuring forth and remaining loyal to the wild in nature and in herself. Likewise, we too have an inner wild side, so she reminds us that if we want to experience a sense of freedom, we must learn to use this spirited nature wisely. When the moon is waxing in Sagittarius, this is a time to venture forth, to know where you're going and why. So, Artemis comes into your life to remind you about your own personal road to freedom. And one of her most important messages is that you have the freedom to change your mind, as did Artemis herself, when she chose to save Iphigeneia from death.

Her Message

Enjoy your freedom, but don't trample on others in the process. Artemis asks you to reflect on what freedom actually means to you. The paradox of freedom is that by over-fixating on it, you become a prisoner to it and you cannot live freely. As Artemis knows, the only real freedom is to be found in taking responsibility for your choices. This will give you an empowering sense of liberty.

To Invoke Artemis's Lunar Blessing

To ensure Artemis is with you to encourage you to make your choices freely, invoke her spirit with this blessing.

Bury two pieces of turquoise under a tree in her honour or cover the stones with leaves or weeds. Raise your arms to the sky and say, 'Artemis, in your forest of life, I am as swift as a deer, as noble as a stag, as bold as a boar, and with all that you cherish in nature, please awaken the free spirit within me.'

Leave your stones in place to petition for Artemis to bring you the spirit of freedom.

Themed Oracles

ROMANTIC RELATIONSHIPS

Unconditional love is a quality to treasure and now is the time to make it clear to someone that you need more space and fewer demands made upon you. Freedom is a gift, but so is seeing how to respect and encourage the freedom of others.

LIFE PURPOSE

It is time to accept you need a new departure. Even though you may be resistant to change, moving forward means you will arrive somewhere else and the more adventurous you are now, the more settled you will become.

FAMILY, FRIENDS AND HOME LIFE

There is someone in your social or family circle who seems to be taking the limelight and affecting your own sense of self-esteem. Step outside of your comfort zone to remind yourself that you are self-assured and impressive where it counts.

Morgan Le Fay

Key

Ambiguity.

Oracle

**Life seems to be a riddle and you want to solve it, but the
solution is simple: life is to be lived.**

Myth

It is likely that Morgan le Fay originated from an ancient Celtic
sea goddess named 'Mor', meaning 'sea'. Fay, or sometimes Fey,
is thought to mean 'the fate' or 'the fairie'. It seems her fate was
to become a legendary enchantress, who was a healer, a powerful

witch and – by many accounts – an archetypal femme fatale.

In early myths, Morgan le Fay was one of the nine queens of Avalon and she was a benevolent figure, using her power to heal others. The *Vita Merlini* by Geoffrey of Monmouth, (c. 1150 CE) tells of her carrying a fatally wounded Arthur to Avalon along with the other queens. In a later tale from the thirteenth century, *The Vulgate Cycle*, Morgan was Queen Guinevere's lady-in-waiting and fell in love with the King's nephew, Guiomar. Guinevere, fearful of scandal, put an end to the romance, but Morgan sought revenge by betraying the Queen's affair with Lancelot to King Arthur. She then went in search of Merlin and offered to become his lover if he would teach her how to wield magic. Meanwhile, in Thomas Malory's fifteenth-century *Le Morte d'Arthur*, Morgan fell in love with Lancelot, whom she imprisoned, refusing to release him until the hero became her lover. The end of Morgan's tale sees her returning to Avalon, as a healer for the sleeping Arthur, who will awaken again in the future when the time is right. Morgan's unpredictable, ambivalent nature has continued to entrance and cast a spell over us all as one of the most complex characters in enchantress myths.

Meaning and Wisdom

What are all these different versions and myths telling you? Is it perhaps that the illusion cast by Morgan is, in fact, that of the storytellers and myth-makers? Don't we all tell our own stories according to what we want to believe or what we want others to believe? So, Morgan may be just a handy hook on which we project our own multi-faceted psyche. Writers of these many medieval legends were informed by the patriarchal nature of the world at the time, so it's no surprise that her femininity was considered to be dangerously bewitching (as was Lilith's, see page 93), desirable and ambiguous. As a shapeshifter, Morgan comes to tell you that you too can adapt and shift according to the situation at hand. You don't have to be always fixed in your opinions or desires, nor even in your routines or behaviour. In fact, live a little more in your imagination and less in your logical mindset.

Her Message

Morgan reminds you to stay open, curious, ready to shift gear or change your mind. Make your own magic just by being yourself. Look deep within you and beyond the outer image you convey to the world. We all wear masks, play roles, pretend to be something we're not at times, and Morgan informs you that you can't hide from yourself. Go with your own rhythms and discover your own flow. The waning moon in Gemini is a time for inner reflection, for writing your own myth, for daydreaming. So, listen to Morgan's advice to take time to experience those moments. Morgan helps you to connect with the imaginative, spiritual or intuitive realm, where all is sacred and held out to you, and nothing is held back. If Morgan can be woven into a sea of legends, then you too can weave your way through life by being an ambiguous enchantress. It's time to discover your own hidden mystique.

To Invoke Morgan's Lunar Blessing

Morgan's legacy originates in an ancient sea goddess, so take a bowl of water to represent the sea and, stirring your hand gently around in a clockwise direction, say:

> *Morgan le Fay, fairie queen,*
> *From tangled tales, your truths are seen.*
> *Unlock your power from deepest seas*
> *To make my magic work for me.*

Next, take nine apples and make a circle with them around a white tea-light candle. Say, 'I heal myself and all I love, and bring joy to those who are true to who they are.'

Light the candle, focus on the flame for a few minutes, then blow it out to encourage Morgan's blessing.

Themed Oracles

ROMANTIC RELATIONSHIPS

Are you an enchantress or are you being enchanted? Whatever the case, being under a spell is fine for now, but don't fall into a trap. Be wary of love's illusions, for sometimes they can divert us from our true pathway.

LIFE PURPOSE

You may be indecisive and not know which way you truly want to go. A new opportunity will soon come your way. It may not at first be all that it seems, but realise this is a chance to move forward and know what you truly want.

FAMILY, FRIENDS AND HOME LIFE

There is ambiguity surrounding a friend's long-term goals. Don't deceive yourself that you know all the answers or try to give advice right now. Let them contemplate and soon all will be resolved.

Ishtar

Tradition: Mesopotamian/Akkadian
Symbols: stars, moon, dove, Venus (planet), nature
Lunar cycle: waning moon in Taurus
Sacred crystal: emerald, malachite, rhodochrosite
Keywords: sexuality, passion, sensuality

Key

Pleasure.

Oracle

In lips you are sweet, in pleasure you are clothed in love; gaze now into the mirror, then a past regret will vanish and love will be replenished.

Myth

Although a goddess in her own right (she may be the 'Great Goddess' revered as Astarte in Phoenicia, Aphrodite in Greece and Cybele in Phrygia), scholars believe the myth of Ishtar's descent to the underworld to rescue her lover, Tammuz, is a version of the earlier Sumerian goddess Inanna's myth (see page 136).

Ishtar was the embodiment of the planet Venus, as both the morning and evening star. As such, she was also worshipped in the triad with the sun god, Shamash and the moon god, Sin. Her symbol was an eight-pointed or sixteen-pointed star within a circle. In Akkadian mythology, she was a fertility goddess, who according to one ancient myth opened the womb of all women. She was never associated with motherhood itself, but rather with sexual desire. Ishtar was the protectress of the *houris*, who welcomed male visitors to the temple with sacred sexual rites. Many texts describe her also as the goddess of fate; thus she was responsible for all of life and death. She was worshipped for her pleasure-giving vitality but was known to be ruthlessly cruel to her lovers. In cult rituals to appease her, many of her male followers were emasculated. She was also the goddess of thunderstorms, rain and war, and – after she stole the *me* (a treasury of divine powers) from the god Enki – she became the supreme deity and ruler of all the gods.

Meaning and Wisdom

This multi-faceted goddess, queen of Heaven and Earth, was not to be crossed. Indeed, her contradictory nature is echoed in the symbolic imagery of the morning and evening star. The morning star represents the energies of seduction and desire and the evening star the relinquishing of pleasure and the withdrawal of love. Ishtar is associated with the energy of the waning moon in pleasure-loving Taurus, as her power to give pleasure is equal to her power to swiftly take away that pleasure, if she so desires.

Her Message

Ishtar comes to ask you if you have been disillusioned by a love relationship? Do you dwell on some past regret or wish things had ended differently? Whether you are still bound by memories from the past or simply lost without love, Ishtar tells you that it is time to let go of this past regret and to embrace or rediscover new love, passion and pleasure. You have a right to experience physical and sexual happiness and to reconnect with your sensuality. Ishtar says, be empowered by your secret desires, explore your sexual needs and preferences and liberate yourself from mistrust or self-sabotage, for soon the morning star and the waxing moon will rise to bring you the pleasure you long for.

To Invoke Ishtar's Lunar Blessing

Reach your hands high above your head and, for a few moments, imagine you are drawing down the planet Venus. As it falls gently towards your hands, imagine you have the planet of love, sex and pleasure in your grasp. Now, consider how it will reignite your own flames of desire, your own sexual intentions, your sensual delights, and thank Ishtar for bringing you her passion, her pleasure and her power.

Themed Oracles

ROMANTIC RELATIONSHIPS

Time to open up, free yourself from the chains of expectations and let yourself be loved, cherished and pampered. A fresh spark of sensual delight is about to come your way.

LIFE PURPOSE

Ideas you have recently proposed don't seem to be taken seriously. And a contact, colleague or friend's ambivalence hasn't helped you to make any progress. But with renewed self-belief, you can make it clear where you're going, and why.

FAMILY, FRIENDS AND HOME LIFE

Sensual pleasure isn't just about sex, it's also about using all the senses. It's about the joy that can be found from a room filled with your favourite fragrance. In fact, now is the time to add a touch of the sensual to your home to bring out the hedonist in you.

Ceridwen

Tradition: Welsh/Celtic
Symbols: cauldron, poetry, dawn, *awen*, herbs
Lunar cycle: dark of the moon in Pisces
Sacred crystals: purple fluorite, amethyst
Keywords: inspiration, art, poetry, imagination, transformation

Key

Inspiration.

Oracle

Inspiration may come to you when you least expect it. Take it as an opportunity to transform your life, even if it means giving up something from your past.

Myth

In medieval Welsh legend, Ceridwen was a shapeshifting enchantress and mother of an ugly son, Mordfran, and a beautiful daughter, Creirwy. She is considered to be the Celtic goddess of rebirth, transformation and inspiration and is associated with the dark of the new moon in Pisces. One legend tells that to compensate for her son's ugliness, Ceridwen concocted a magic potion in her cauldron. The potion, known as *awen*, would bestow the gift of poetic inspiration and wisdom upon him. The cauldron had to be stirred for a year and a day and only the first three drops were magical. Gwion, a young boy servant, was ordered to stir the elixir, but the three precious drops of burning liquid spilled onto his thumb. Instinctively he put his thumb to his mouth to cool it down and he gained the wisdom and knowledge Ceridwen had intended for her son. Gwion fled, but in her fury, Ceridwen sought revenge, shapeshifting into different forms and chasing Gwion through the skies and seas, before eventually swallowing the boy. Gwion was then reborn as the sixth-century Welsh bard, Taliesin, who is believed to have sung at the courts of at least three kings. In medieval times, Taliesin became a mythic hero and was thought to have been King Arthur's companion. The *Book of Taliesin*, which dates from the fourteenth century, includes work that is believed to have been written many centuries earlier. The book is filled with verses about *awen* as the inspiration of poets and includes mysterious lines thought to be an oracle.

Meaning and Wisdom

Ceridwen represents the power of inspired transformation; a change from one process to another, akin to alchemy, or the ending of one cycle and the beginning of a new one. Similarly, the dark of the moon in Pisces is a time when the depths of our own magical inspiration can rise to the surface and change our perception of the world. Creativity is an alchemical process too – a flash of inspiration may come from nowhere and then you must do something with it, to turn your lead into gold.

As you have chosen Ceridwen, you are likely in the process of some form of metamorphosis. Are you looking to give up something in your life and discover something better? Do you long to be more creative or find inspiration? Ceridwen brings you her divine magic and asks you: first, what is your intention? If you know it, act upon your vision. Second, if you don't know, are you ready to taste the *awen* and be inspired? And thirdly, if the answer is yes, then it's time to open yourself up and let the divine power flow through you.

Her Message

Ceridwen is here to help you be inspired, to showcase your talents or be motivated to carry on regardless. She is here to enrich and inform you with her creative power and to tell you that now you are ready to take on a new role or lead others to see their own potential. Three drops of magical wisdom are now yours to take from the elixir held out to you in a cup of gold. But who holds the cup? In other words, is it an external opportunity or is it your own goblet of creativity? Imagine tasting only three drops and, regardless of who holds the cup, you are now ready to be inspired.

To Invoke Ceridwen's Lunar Blessing

Ceridwen's crystals are amethyst and purple fluorite, both linking you to her higher wisdom. Hold a piece of either crystal to your third eye (the middle of your forehead just above the bridge of your nose) and say, 'Welcome, Ceridwen. Deep within me, I can turn my inspiration to creative purpose and I will now manifest my goal.' Leave the crystal in a box or dark place for one lunar cycle for the magic to work.

Themed Oracles

ROMANTIC RELATIONSHIPS

You have the chance to transform your relationship for the better. This is a time to listen to your heart and establish new projects if attached, or if single, form new bonds or see what's on offer.

LIFE PURPOSE

You are now inspired to make the changes you were hoping for, even though others may not be in agreement with you. For once, shift your perception, see how you may have been denying what you can really achieve and make it clear you know where you're going and why.

FAMILY, FRIENDS AND HOME LIFE

There may be someone in your family or social life who is charismatic and motivated but is stealing your limelight. Soon you will be able to make a powerful impression where it counts and be centre stage again.

Persephone

Tradition: Ancient Greece
Symbols: pomegranate, ear of wheat, grain, the
    four seasons
Lunar cycle: dark of the moon in Virgo
Sacred crystals: rainbow tourmaline, clear quartz crystal
Keywords: purification, fertility, stillness, rhythm,
    cycle, flow

Key

Alignment.

Oracle

Go with the flow of the natural cycles around you to bring you closer to your sacred self. Making magic is about believing in yourself and, if you can do that, you can make anything happen.

Myth

Persephone, like Inanna (see page 135), is another goddess who descended to the underworld – but not of her own volition. Also known as Kore, meaning 'maiden' in Ancient Greek, Persephone – daughter of Earth goddess, Demeter, and sky god, Zeus – was both queen of the underworld and goddess of spring and was worshipped alongside Demeter in the cult of the Eleusinian Mysteries, which promised the initiate a blessed afterlife. Persephone was abducted by the god of the underworld, Hades, to be his consort, while she was out picking flowers in the meadows. Demeter searched for her daughter everywhere, but to no avail. It was only with the help of Hecate's flaming torch that Persephone was eventually discovered.

When Demeter discovered that Zeus had told Hades where to snatch Persephone, Demeter withheld all fertility on the Earth as an act of revenge. The gods realised that they had to restore fertility or humankind would never worship them. But Persephone had been tricked into eating Hades's pomegranate seeds in the underworld, which meant she was bound forever to spend a part of the year with him. As a compromise, it was agreed with Hades that Persephone would spend the other half of the year with her mother. Her annual return to Earth in spring was marked by growth, fertility and joy. When she descended to the underworld at harvest time, her departure marked the winter season and a time of recuperation.

Meaning and Wisdom

Persephone reminds us to wake up each day with a smile on our face, knowing that another day is another chance to start afresh or revise our goals. She aligns with the dark of the new moon in Virgo, when we may sense the end of summer is a threat to our joy rather than a positive change. So, Persephone represents the end of summer and the changing seasons. Persephone asks you to think about your own rhythms and cycles. Do you go with the flow or fight against it? Do you find each morning a joy or a test? This spring and winter goddess of the underworld reminds you of all your ups and downs and how to shift gracefully between them. Perhaps now is the time to awaken to the spring, summer, autumn and winter within you.

Her Message

How in touch are you with your own cycles and are you connecting with those of nature and the universe? Persephone rises from the underworld to lead you to see the magic of the seasons. To align to the cycles of the moon, the sun, the planets and nature, to see that every time you choose to go with the flow, you are no longer wrapped up in the past, but ready to move with the present. To see that you have an outer life that you project into the world and an inner life that only you truly know. When Persephone comes into your life, she asks you to respect both and to open yourself up to the rhythms and flow of the universe.

To Invoke Persephone's Lunar Blessing

Persephone rules the dark, so to connect to her power, light a candle in a darkened place then blow it straight out. As you are suddenly plunged into darkness, call on Persephone to protect and purify you by saying, 'Take all of nature in your care during the dark of winter, revive the world at springtime, and keep my soul aligned to all that is within and without me.'

Themed Oracles

ROMANTIC RELATIONSHIPS

Your emotions may be dancing to a different rhythm than someone else's, but that doesn't mean you're not compatible or out of sync. You will soon discover a way to achieve harmony and understanding, through finding a mutual goal or meaning in life.

LIFE PURPOSE

You recently saw the way to shine a new light down a murky road of possible success, but you hesitated and didn't take the chance. You are now more than ever willing to try again. During the next lunar cycle, rekindle your motivation.

FAMILY, FRIENDS AND HOME LIFE

Consolidation is needed so that you have time to plan ahead and make decisions for your home, friends or family. Taking time to weigh all the pros and cons will pay off and rethinking the possibilities will give you a burst of energy to get cracking when the time is right.

Coyolxāuhqui

Tradition: Aztec/Mexico
Symbols: gold, bells, earrings, eagle feathers, fire
  serpent
Lunar cycle: dark of the moon in Aries
Sacred crystals: green tourmaline, turquoise
Keywords: defeat, disappointment, regrouping,
  foresight

Key

Setback.

Oracle

**When dark clouds hang heavy in the night air, you will
find that rising above them brings you the clarity of the
star-filled heavens.**

Myth

Aztec myth tells of the goddess Coyolxāuhqui, who was butchered
by her brother Huītzilīpīchtli, the god of war. Coyolxāuhqui's head
was tossed into the sky and became the moon.

The story begins with Coyolxāuhqui's mother, the Earth goddess Cōātlīcue tending to her shrine. Suddenly, a ball of hummingbird feathers fell from the sky (perhaps a euphemism!) and Cōātlīcue picked it up and placed it by her waist. From this she fell pregnant. The rebellious Coyolxāuhqui was furious that her mother had conceived a child by shameful means and she led her 400 brothers in an attempt to kill their mother. Sensing the danger his mother was in, the embryo sprang from Cōātlīcue's womb as the fully grown, invincible warrior, Huītzilīpīchtli. He carried a lightning-like weapon known as the *Xiuhcoatl* ('fire serpent'), with which he slaughtered all of his siblings, dismembering Coyolxāuhqui and throwing her limbs down a mountainside. He finally tossed her head into the sky, where she became the moon and her brothers the stars.

This story was commemorated in a celebrated relief stone found at the foot of the sacrificial pyramid Templo Mayor in the Aztec capital Tenochtitlan.

Meaning and Wisdom

Although this bloodthirsty story sounds very far from the positive influence of lunar power, it reflects the qualities associated with the dark of the new moon in Aries. This is a period when our power feels as if it is taken away from us and we struggle to retain or reclaim it. We become convinced we are champions for a cause, act without thinking of the consequences and may discover that we are wrong. There will be times when we are defeated or disappointed, our feelings dismembered, our heads and hearts no longer working in tandem and we feel like everything's gone wrong. But with any kind of setback, we can also reflect and review, turn our heads to the sky and see the bigger picture. It's when we let defeat trammel us into the ground, when we don't pick up our own pieces, that we end up victims of our own apathy or despair. So, this goddess tells you to hold your head up as high as the moon and look to the future.

Her Message

Coyolxāuhqui comes to tell you to accept a recent setback as nothing more than an opportunity to review your situation. This warrior goddess was brave enough to stand up for her beliefs, even at the cost of her siblings' lives. Her message is both to rebel and have faith in what you believe in, but don't sacrifice other people's hopes and dreams. With foresight and prescience, you don't have to suffer disappointment, for the latter only comes if your own or other people's expectations are too high. The bells that hang around Coyolxāuhqui's face are perhaps tinkling, jangling reminders telling you not to leap into battle too fast without seeing what the outcome might be.

To Invoke Coyolxāuhqui's Lunar Blessing

Ask Coyolxāuhqui for strength and positive energy for healing and to resolve any setbacks or problems. Look up to the moon and say, 'Dear moon goddess, send me the power of your blessing, so that I may rise again to take centre-stage in my own sky.'

Themed Oracles

ROMANTIC RELATIONSHIPS

You now have the foresight to see where a relationship is going and whether you need to hold back or press onwards. Don't prevaricate; action will bring you the results you truly desire.

LIFE PURPOSE

It's not that you feel defeated, but more weak-minded and uncertain of your next move. Soon you will feel strong, determined and ready to leap into action, but for now, stand back, retreat a little and you'll soon have a more objective outlook.

FAMILY, FRIENDS AND HOME LIFE

Don't go to war with others over a silly disagreement. Think about why it matters so much to get your point across or defend your cause. Is it because you know you are right, or just that you hate to be proved wrong? This is now the time to lay down your weapons and find a way to agree to differ.

Conclusion

Inscribed on a stone at the Temple of Delphi, the home of Apollo's oracle, the Pythia, is a simple maxim, 'Know Thyself.'

It is in the spirit of this most powerful of messages that the lunar oracles in this book have been sent to you. 'Know Thyself' was interpreted by Plato in the fourth century BCE to mean 'know your soul', and by connecting with the moon's soulful energy you can begin to know your sacred self.

To seek self-knowledge is a life-long quest, a journey of discovery and not a destination. It is through developing self-knowledge and self-understanding that you can live out your potential and encourage the lifestyle, love and happiness that give you meaning in life. These messages not only mirror who you are right now, but show you more clearly who you are becoming.

These oracles open your soul's eyes to see what you might need to know at any given moment on your self-knowledge journey. And it is with these empowering messages to *know thyself* that you can begin to glimpse the hidden mysteries within you.

These lunar oracles are a reflection of all that you are, so look within, again and again, and find yourself.

The Zodiac Lunar Phases
and Corresponding Characters

Aries

Waxing moon – The Morrígan (see 171)
Full moon – Mama Killa (see 27)
Waning moon – Ix Chel (see 231)
Dark of the moon – Coyolxāuhqui (see 297)

Taurus

Waxing moon – Medb (see 243)
Full moon – Gaia (see 51)
Waning moon – Ishtar (see 279)
Dark of the moon – Circe (see 177)

Gemini

Waxing moon – Diana (see 195)
Full moon – Yèmoja (see 189)

Waning moon – Mohini (see 249)
Dark of the moon – Morgan le Fay (see 273)

Cancer

Waxing moon – Bendis (see 15)
Full moon – Nut (see 21)
Waning moon – Thetis (see 255)
Dark of the moon – Nyx (see 219)

Leo

Waxing moon – The Sibyl (see 237)
Full moon – Brigid (see 75)
Waning moon – Dido (see 207)
Dark of the moon – Inanna (see 135)

Virgo

Waxing moon – Hina (see 147)
Full moon – Britomartis (see 117)
Waning moon – Mélusine (see 159)
Dark of the moon – Persephone (see 291)

Libra

Waxing moon – Rhiannon (see 69)
Full moon – Dewi Ratih (see 39)
Waning moon – Calypso (see 153)
Dark of the moon – Hecate (see 57)

Scorpio

Waxing moon – Isis (see 111)
Full moon – Selene (see 225)
Waning moon – Frigg (see 183)
Dark of the moon – Kali (see 33)

Sagittarius

Waxing moon – Artemis (see 267)
Full moon – Luna (see 213)
Waning moon – Devana (see 165)
Dark of the moon – Lilith (see 93)

Capricorn

Waxing moon – Awilix (see 45)
Full moon – Triple Goddess (see 81)
Waning moon – Tārā (see 63)
Dark of the moon – The Cailleach (see 261)

Aquarius

Waxing moon – The Vile (see 105)
Full moon – Arianrhod (see 99)
Waning moon – Pasiphaë (see 129)
Dark of the moon – Blodeuwedd (see 123)

About the author

Sarah Bartlett is a professional astrologer and illustrator, and the author of *The Little Book of Magic* series, *The Wiccan Almanac*, *The Book of Enchanted Living* and *The Tarot Bible*. Sarah lives in the countryside, where she practises natural magic and other esoteric arts.

Pisces

Waxing moon – Chang'e (see 141)
Full moon – Hanwi (see 201)
Waning moon – Nimue (see 87)
Dark of the moon – Ceridwen (see 285)